IRINA

In 1983, Irina Ratushinskaya, one of Russia's
leading poets, was sentenced to twelve years in a strict-
regime prison camp. Her crime was 'anti-Soviet agitation
in the form of poetry'.

In prison, she was kept in degrading conditions.
Her diet was bread and water, with rotten cabbage soup
every other day. Her hair was shaved off. She spent
months at a time isolated in the punishment cell, with
only a few thin clothes to protect her against the sub-zero
temperatures. Her husband, Igor, began to plead for her
release.

His pleas were heard in England by Dick Rodgers,
a surgeon and priest living in Birmingham. Like many
others, he lobbied for Irina's release. But unlike others,
he spent forty-six days in a cell matching Irina's to bring
her plight before the eyes of the Western world.

This is the story of what happened when a group of
determined individuals confronted a superpower.

To Sue, Christopher and Timothy

Irina

DICK RODGERS

A LION PAPERBACK
Tring • Batavia • Sydney

Copyright © 1987 Keston College

Published by
Lion Publishing plc
Icknield Way, Tring, Herts, England
ISBN 0 7459 1367 9
Lion Publishing Corporation
1705 Hubbard Avenue, Batavia, Illinois 60510, USA
ISBN 0 7459 1367 9
Albatross Books Pty Ltd
PO Box 320, Sutherland, NSW 2232, Australia
ISBN 0 86760 922 2

First edition 1987

Acknowledgments
Cover photo: Keston College, Heathfield Road, Keston, Kent

Printed and bound in Great Britain by Cox and Wyman, Reading

CONTENTS

PREFACE

Irina was in prison—a prison within a prison. She was ill-clad, starving, cold and ill. There was no way out. Around her prison brooded high barbed-wire fences, an electrified fence, dogs, arc-lights, guards and guns. Access to the prison was by a railway line flanked by the graves of its builders. Irina's husband a thousand miles away feared for her life. So too did her fellow prisoners. Death was no stranger there. Amnesty International reports that in one year, that same camp claimed 135 lives.

I had no alternative but to heed her husband's cry for help. I spent Lent 1986 in a makeshift 'cell' to help people identify with her, and subsequently I continued campaigning for her release. My four-year-old son, Christopher, was intrigued.

'Daddy,' he pondered, 'why doesn't the Russian government give Irina the right bit of paper to come to England?'

So we asked them, and they gave it to her—eventually.

Out she came, out past the electric fence, the dogs, the lights, the guns, the graves. She came to have tea with my parents in London. She sat on their sofa and drank their tea. She and her husband played with Christopher. They walked in the woods. And when they woke up the next morning at their hosts' house and drew the curtain, it was still London. It wasn't a dream! She came to my home town and a thousand came to meet her. They loved her. They hugged and kissed her and mobbed her with flowers.

These last eighteen months I've lived through a miracle. When I think what's happened, I still get a lump in my throat.

I don't think anyone can claim to have 'got Irina out of

prison'. You never know what goes on behind the scenes, or whose contribution it was that finally tipped the balance. Many organizations and thousands of individuals worked and wept and campaigned and prayed for her release, and at great cost to themselves. They must all share in some measure the joy I feel at having witnessed this remarkable event.

Irina knew what she had to do. She had to be true to the truth. She knew it would cost her dearly but she made up her mind never to waver, never to compromise. She was loyal to her friends in prison, her husband and her God. She did it all with precision, giving the KGB no answers, jealously guarding the morale of her prisoner friends and defending them time and again. She's a heroine. And she's also very human. She was afraid, but her courage was such that God gave her strength to overcome her fears and keep control of herself.

Without the faithfulness of Igor, her husband, she would not be here today. He wrote to her. He pleaded for support most eloquently. He endured the grief of endless visits to the KGB and endless journeys to the camp, only to be turned away time and again.

Some credit must also go to the Soviet government for allowing themselves to be persuaded to release Irina eight years early, and to Mr Gorbachev whose decision this clearly was.

On this side of the East-West divide the work for Irina's release was very much a team effort.

First and foremost, I am indebted to my wife, Sue, for letting me do all this and for putting up with all the heartache and inconvenience of my absence. She has coped with the uncertainty of the step I took, leaving my surgical career to take up freelance work full time, promoting interest in the plight of religious believers in communist countries. It has cost a bit but we are happier now than we've ever been.

Christopher, our son, shared the cost too. I asked him yesterday what he thought of my time in the cage. 'I missed you a lot,' he admitted, 'but I did enjoy playing there. I got into your cage once, do you remember? You had a little boy in your cage!' I don't think it's done him any permanent damage. When Irina came to Birmingham, he could hardly believe his eyes. He stood in the aisle in front of Irina as the crowds washed past him, simply gazing at her in a trance! At one stage he told me: 'It's a good thing you're doing at the moment, Daddy!' Praise indeed from a four-year-old!

The family has been terrific. Mum and Dad turned out to nearly everything. Nothing was too much trouble for them. My sister, Mary, and her family live near us in Birmingham and worked tirelessly at the cell and in the office. Sue and Liz, my other sisters, live further afield but lent very valuable support.

Without Keston College, the research centre where they receive news from religious believers in Eastern Europe, I'd never have heard of Irina. Their service is a real lifeline. Royalties for the sale of this book will be used to support the work of Keston College. Although we depended heavily on Keston College for our information, I should make it clear that the College did not campaign for Irina's release. As an educational charity, it is not its place to do so. If it did, it would lose the necessary academic distance, and its information would cease to be non-partisan.

It has been a joy to work alongside Amnesty International and the Bukovsky Institute. I applaud this professionalism and gratefully acknowledge Amnesty's provision of details about Irina's camp and the Institute's publication of a copy of the diary kept by the women prisoners. I am also indebted to an ex-prisoner, Avraham Shifrin, who has collated some amazing details about the camps of the Gulag in his *First Guidebook to the USSR — to prisons and concentration camps of the Soviet Union.*

I'm very grateful to the Irina Vigil committee for making sure that the whole venture stayed on the rails and for working so hard at it.

Thank you, John Wesson, the rector of St Martin's Church in Birmingham's Bull Ring, which welcomed me and my cage, and thanks to the congregation and the 'Beadles' who helped so much in many practical ways. I'm grateful to my own church, St David's, Shenley Green, and to all the other hundred or more people who helped in the office, at the cage or by keeping Sue company or in a thousand other ways.

Thanks too to all the media, politicians and church leaders who helped towards Irina's release, especially to my own Bishop, Hugh Montefiore, and to Tim Renton, the Minister at the Foreign Office.

Alyona Kojevnikov of Keston College kept in touch by telephone with Igor and eventually with Irina, in Kiev. So it was particularly appreciated that Alyona and her husband, Kolya, and son, Alex, opened their home to Irina and Igor while they were in London.

I was very conscious of a massive team effort all over the world devoted to the goal of Irina's release. Many participants were in action before I was. Bloodaxe Books were already preparing a book of her poetry entitled *No, I'm not Afraid*, with the excellent translations by David McDuff which are used in this book, with his kind permission. The poets and writers of the world took up her defence with the Poetry Society in London and International PEN (the association of writers) very much to the fore. The *Missjon bak Jernteppet* (Mission behind the Iron Curtain) in Norway seemed to lead the field of the European organizations working for Irina, together with the Bukovsky Institute of Amsterdam, the *Action Chretienne pour l'Abolition de la Torture* and *Aide aux Chretiens en Russie*, which are based in Paris; the *Centro Russia Christiana* of Milan, Christian Solidarity International in Zurich, and a whole host of organizations and individuals in the United States, Australia and New Zealand. USSR News Brief in Munich kept closely in touch with the situation and Amnesty International adopted her and organized several special actions for her.

Many helped financially, although we have almost always been nearly broke, usually having to press ahead with projects and worry about the money later.

I'm grateful for their tolerance to those whom I may have offended, including any glaring omissions from these credits. My thanks to Irina and to Bob Gillette for the first-hand accounts in Chapter One, to the long-suffering Metropolitan and and West Midlands Police forces, to the interpreters Alyona Kojevnikov, Jane Ellis and Professor Geoffrey Hosking and to my Icelandic hosts, Oscar, Inmar,

Agnethe, Gudni and the Bjarnarrssons.

Sergei Lavrov, the diplomat at the Soviet Embassy in London, and Mr Prosvirin in Reykjavik, both received me courteously and seem to have conveyed my concerns to their seniors effectively. I am grateful to them and also to Mr Shevardnardze, who seems to have reported back after our encounter on the streets of London.

It's been a joy having the help of my secretary, Sarah Wylie, who worked cheerfully and efficiently throughout. She met the deadline and enthused enough about the story to keep me going!

I don't know how to include God in the credits. One day rushing about London in my dog collar, on a campaigning errand, I dashed across a side street in front of a mail van. The cockney driver leant out and expostulated with me in that friendly way they have, 'If you do that again, mate, you'll be going to see your Governor!' That's what he's been. It was all his idea in the first place and he's been a marvellous boss to work for.

The recorded speech in this book represents the gist of what was said rather than being a series of verbatim accounts.

1

THE PUPPET THEATRE

If you go for a tourist trip to Moscow, don't feel that you have to go on all the excursions; just go out in the street and wander around. One of the places you must see is *GUM*, the State Universal department store in the centre of the city. It's a cross between Crystal Palace and the Ideal Home Exhibition, built in Tsarist times for lots of little market traders.

Going out of the front door, you're on Red Square, facing the crenellated wall of the Kremlin. In front of the wall, flanked by grandstands for official dignitaries, squats a gaunt, rectangular, granite mausoleum. Even on winter days, there's always a queue of a hundred or more Soviet citizens waiting to file past Lenin's body to pay their respects. On the left rise the brightly painted towers and domes of St Basil's Cathedral, and on the right the more mundane edifice which houses the History Museum.

Five minutes up Gorky Street and you see on your right the armour-clad equestrian statue of the founder of Moscow—Yuri Dolgoruki—as he brandishes his shield and sword. Five more minutes will take you to Pushkin Square, where the great poet hangs his head amid a pleasantly appointed garden in front of the Rossia cinema.

Not far away you'll find the Puppet Theatre is a notable Moscow meeting place. On a cool afternoon in the autumn of 1981, its electronic chimes were ringing out. If you'd been there, you might have noticed a young couple, standing waiting near the clock. The woman, in her late twenties, was slightly built. She had a melancholy Slavic face, but when she smiled up at her husband her face was clear, as if she had nothing to hide. Her husband was looking out for someone.

A man appeared from a doorway on the far side of the street. He came from a dreary, yellow building, built by German prisoners of war, which housed foreign correspondents and their families. A young woman walked with him. When they got to a point just opposite the Puppet Theatre, they disappeared down the subway to emerge for the rendezvous under the clock. Five foot ten and clean-shaven with brown hair and gold glasses, Bob Gillette was one year into his posting as Moscow correspondent of the *Los Angeles Times*. His companion, an American woman, had been nanny to the families of other expatriates in Moscow before working for the Gillettes. He was glad of her help in understanding the finer points of any conversation with this couple who had sought him out.

He had been a bit curt with them on the telephone, but he had to be with unknown callers in Moscow. He didn't know how they had got hold of his telephone number. There are no official directories of private numbers in circulation in the Soviet Union, and Directory Enquiries simply refuses to give out the numbers of Westerners, at least to native Russian speakers. However, an English language directory (*Information Moscow*) is published for foreigners by the Official Soviet Journalist, Victor Louis, and his British wife, Jennifer and copies circulate in dissident circles.

The Puppet Theatre was a convenient, but not very discreet, meeting place. It was much over-used by correspondents, and so probably under steady surveillance. At least the roar of traffic discouraged voice pick-up.

Bob was distracted with other work at the time, a bit impatient and, as always, suspicious. At least once a week some caller would plead with him, usually to beg for help in emigrating or finding a decent place to live or righting some notable wrong. Almost invariably, there was nothing a foreigner could do to help. Sometimes they appeared to be straightforward provocateurs, like the weasely little man who once asked him to help him get money and weapons to carry out acts of anti-communist terror. (Maybe he was serious. Who knows?) These thoughts were going through his mind as they chatted, sizing each other up.

14

The woman under the clock was Irina Ratushinskaya, from Odessa on the Black Sea. Her husband was Igor Gerashchenko, a physicist from Kiev. Both in their late twenties, they had been married for two years. As is usual in the Soviet Union, she had retained her maiden name.

In an attempt to be more discreet, they strolled among the trees in the little park at the side of the theatre. Irina introduced herself as a poet. 'Oh no, not another one who wants her stuff smuggled to the West,' thought Bob Gillette. She was almost completely unknown at the time, except to a tiny community of largely dissident intellectuals who had managed to read her poetry unofficially, or listen to it through the screech of jammers on foreign radio. Some of her work evidently had already reached the West. But as it turned out, they didn't really seem to want anything from him, except to make contact for future reference. She seemed sweet and modest, which was not in Bob's experience a common trait among Russian artists. She was also a bit shy, with large melancholy brown eyes. Igor, a head taller than Irina, had a deep, penetrating gaze, and stood by rather protectively. It became obvious later that he had good reason to be protective. They were being harassed by the Ukrainian KGB, whose methods made the Moscow branch of the Security Police seem positively soft and easy-going.

On 10 December, Igor and Irina telephoned Bob again. The date was memorable —it is United Nations Human Rights Day, the occasion for *Pravda*'s annual editorial, congratulating the Soviet Union for its superlative human-rights achievements, and excoriating the West for its cynical claims to non-existent liberties. It is also the annual occasion for a sad little demonstration in Pushkin Square on Gorky Street, where small numbers of people seek to pay tribute to Andrei Sakharov and others by simply standing near Pushkin's statue in silence. The few who dare to doff their hats are immediately detained by plain-clothes police.

It was grey twilight and very cold when Irina and Igor appeared outside the Puppet Theatre that day. They had managed to evade surveillance at the railway station in

Kiev, and had come to Moscow for the sole purpose of standing for an hour or so in bitter cold by the statue of Russia's most revered poet. She asked the journalist to follow them as they approached the Square, about a fifteen-minute walk through spitting snow, and to let friends know if they were arrested. She gave him a small scrap of paper with a first name and a Moscow telephone number on it.

As they walked across the broad plaza in front of Izvestia's editorial offices on Gorky Street, the journalist dropped about fifty feet behind them at Igor's suggestion. A gust of freezing wind smacked him in the face. In the moment it took to wipe the tears away and clear his vision, they disappeared. He assumed they had gone across the side street to the Square, but as he approached it, he could see that this was not likely. The Square was virtually surrounded by plain-clothes agents, all of them wearing similar sheepskin coats, plaid mufflers and a characteristic look of bland arrogance.

One of them stopped him and demanded to know where he was going. The American asked him who he was. He snapped open a little leather-bound booklet identifying him as an officer of the KGB.

'What's going on?' asked the American.

The Russian replied, with a grin that suggested no pretence of truth, that 'a dangerous criminal' was on the loose. He let him go when he claimed to be a tourist en route to the National Hotel a few blocks further on. Gillette circled round, walked unopposed through a side entrance into Pushkin Square, and settled down on an ice-covered bench.

Forty minutes later, he had melted a depression in the ice and turned numb from the waist down, but still no Igor or Irina. He went off to a telephone box to make the call.

About ten days later, having served a standard 'administrative' sentence (a summary sentence without trial), for petty hooliganism (the rough equivalent of what we would call 'disturbing the peace'), they telephoned again and arranged to meet at the 'usual place', without mentioning the Puppet Theatre on the phone. This little precaution had no effect. The journalist arrived a few minutes early to find one of the clumsiest displays of street surveillance he

16

had ever seen. Half a dozen men of similar age, build, attire and affected nonchalance strolled aimlessly back and forth in front of the Puppet Theatre. Plainly, they were not waiting for a bus because buses came and went and they remained. At one point the squad's apparent leader gave furtive little hand signals to the others who re-distributed themselves in front of the Theatre. Perhaps this was all meant as a form of intimidation.

Irina and Igor soon arrived on a bus, trailed by at least two more agents. One was carrying a cheap, black briefcase which he kept aiming towards the little group. Did it contain a peep-hole camera? Irina and her husband seemed totally uninhibited by all this. As they walked a meandering route through the back streets, the gang of gumshoes flitted behind and ahead and across the street like cockroaches on the kitchen floor. On the way they talked animatedly about their brief jail terms, the awful food, the miserable conditions and the fascinating people they had met in jail. She had been in Butyrki Prison, a mile away in the north-west part of the city, and Igor had been outside the city limits at a workcamp with the poetic name of *The Birches*. The American still hadn't figured it all out. Who were they? What were they about? They were two strangers from Kiev who seemed excited about having been thrown in jail for conspiring to stand next to Pushkin's statue in total silence on the significant day of 10 December. He still hadn't read a word of Irina's poetry and didn't know anyone who had. Obscurity, of course, is no gauge of talent in the Soviet Union—often quite the reverse as Irina was to prove.

As they skulked in the back streets of Moscow, he still couldn't dispel the lingering suspicion that this intense young couple might be playing a role in some quaint little drama. Could it all have been scripted by the police to make him look like a subversive Western agent? The line between prudence and paranoia is a fuzzy one, and this would not have been the crudest Soviet preparation for entrapment on record. Afterwards, he could see the couple's loquacious excitement in another light. Perhaps it was a mixture of fear and the exhilaration of having stood up for deeply held principles. They, or she, had set out on a course which was to lead them into a moral confrontation with the Soviet state. The inevitable consequences were plain to them. It seemed as if Igor had set himself the task of shielding Irina from these consequences as long as he could, and when that was no longer possible, he concentrated on preserving her work.

The clock on the Puppet Theatre is a pretty little sight and an official guide would be happy to direct you to it. However, it's unlikely that directions would be quite so forthcoming for a place less than a mile away, where Irina spent ten unforgettable days.

The Puppet Theatre is just over a mile due north of Red Square. Face the Puppet Clock, and then turn left, 500 yards along there, at the end of a little garden which flanks the Garden Ring, and before you get to Gorky Street again, turn right. You're on your own now. It might be indiscreet to ask directions. About ten minutes walk up there, just before it becomes Butyrki Street and near the Savolyevski Station stands an anonymous building which is part of another world. To be precise, it is Moscow's Special Reception Centre Number Two, next door to the Butyrki Prison at 45 Novoslobodskaya Street. This became Irina's home for the rest of her winter visit.

The other prisoners were taken to work in a factory nearby for a full eight-hour day, every day including Saturdays and Sundays. The factory was given the intriguing name of *Freedom*. In the evening they had to work in the Reception Centre, clearing up after the warders' drinking parties. There were a lot of these in the run-up to the New Year festivities.

The freedom of the factory was denied to Irina. She was kept in the Reception Centre each day, as the other women left for work, in a cell on the ground floor with a grille over the window and a plank for a bed. She used to feed the sparrows through the grille. They became her friends. She heard no familiar noises of city life—no trains leaving for the upper reaches of the Volga from the station nearby; no Number 3, 23 or 47 trams outside in the street; no bells from the Moscow churches.

Most Muscovite households need the mother to go out to work for financial reasons, which means leaving their

18

children in a nursery. A ten-day sentence is financially very damaging to these women, since they lose both their regular pay and the incentive payments on which they depend. They try to make up for their loss by pilfering from the factory. The guards searched the prisoners as they went back into the Reception Centre. Irina was pretty quick to deduce that they turned a blind eye to a lot of the stuff which they discovered. They seemed to want the pilfering to continue.

At the same time, there were some obvious hiding-places in the cell which were rarely searched. For instance, there was a ventilation shaft covered by a little door. The inside had been bricked up and didn't lead anywhere. All the guards had to do was wait till it was full. On one search, Irina saw two warders go off with fifty pounds' worth of cosmetics, which seemed to be about par for the course. The prisoners surmised that the cosmetics did not end up back in the factory, but somehow got lost on the way. Her cell-mates were very irritated at having been caught in this fashion, so they tried to make sure that the next batch of prisoners didn't meet with the same fate; they bent the flimsy wooden door which had closed the entrance of the duct and made it seem such a good hiding-place. Once the guards saw the door wouldn't close any more, there was a terrible commotion. The supervisors in turn all tried to fix the door. In the middle of the night they called out the joiner to repair it, paint it and then scratch it slightly so that the new paint wouldn't be quite so noticeable. It was an unprecedented job. By comparison, the water boiler in the kitchen had been out of order for a month and nobody seemed to bother about it.

The warders held a 'book of prisoners' comments'. Every one was overflowing with gratitude: for attention to hygiene, medical care, courteous treatment, mental welfare and finally, re-education. What's it all about? How did they get these comments? The method is simple. At the end of ten days, they lead you to believe that the police are coming to take you away for further processing.

'But what for?'

'Oh, you'll see when you get there.'

19

They make you wait for hours stewing in your own thoughts and doubts. Then it becomes clear that whether the police come or not depends on the outcome of a telephone call. Then all of a sudden the phone rings, they come over to you, haul you out to the exit—and tell you there won't be any police coming for you—you can go!

'Just before you go, wouldn't you like to write a word of thanks in our visitors' book?'

And of course you're ready to put anything they want.

The hygiene arrangements were simple. The only tap produced icy cold water. Two cells (about forty-five people) were herded into a toilet where the tap was. You had ten minutes in which to do your best. There was supposed to be a shower for new arrivals—to make them 'hygienic'—but Irina hardly discovered anybody who had ever managed to get it.

It was really cold in the cells, and almost everyone was ill, but there wasn't any point going to the doctor. Any time spent in the sick bay was extra to the days of your sentence. They wouldn't even give you tablets, because it was considered dangerous to drug the prisoners—even with cough medicine.

Most of the women were prepared to put up with any kind of indignity in order to avoid getting their sentence extended. According to the rules, arguing with a warder got you an extra thirty days. When Irina was there, there was a seventy-year-old woman who would always stand up when a young guard came into the cell. That's how things were; these were 'the rules'. When Irina failed to stand up, the guards preferred not to notice. There was an old woman in her cell who failed to stand up when they came round for the morning head count. She simply hadn't woken up. Consequently, they kept her back so that she missed a day at work, prolonging her sentence by a day.

'Come on, Granny,' they shouted. 'We'll teach you to stand up.'

They took her away to another cell beyond earshot. She returned in the evening very tearful, not wanting to talk about what had happened.

The cell measured twenty square metres, about twelve

feet by fifteen feet, much the same as the double bedroom in the Birmingham suburban semi where my wife and I live. Judging by the racks for soap and toothbrushes, the cell was intended for sixteen people. Most cells had twenty to twenty-five people in them, sleeping on boards around the wall and on the floor. Apparently at the time of the Olympics there were sixty to a cell.

Over the New Year they tried to take less. The guards like to have their parties around then and the fewer people in the cell, the better. On the other hand, the police get paid £2.50 for each arrest and they need the cash over the New Year.

It's a shame that the Puppet Theatre Clock only has an electronic chime. It's not as loud as London's Bow Bells. If it were, the women in the Reception Centre would have been able to tell the time by it. After all, it's less than a mile away.

2

INTRODUCING IRINA

The plight of Irina Ratushinskaya first came to my attention on a November morning in 1985 when a brown envelope dropped through the door of my Birmingham home.

It came from Keston College, a research centre near Bromley in Kent. Here, some fifteen to twenty specialists in East European languages monitor the situation of religious believers in communist countries. They get their information by reading *Pravda* and other official newspapers, as well as from a large number of unofficially published documents which are typed on thin paper and brought to the West by a variety of different means. These often report the arrest of Jewish or Christian activists, people who have published magazines, run a Sunday school, administered a fund for the relief of the poor, or been engaged in anything that the state considers to be an 'anti-Soviet activity'. They aim to put this information in context in order to help people understand the situation of the church as a whole. It's an independent body, not government or church-sponsored, and it continues to play an extremely important role.

If I were arrested in Moscow for running a Sunday school, as does happen, it would be no small comfort to my wife to think that she could get a report about my arrest through to somebody in the West who would understand and publish it. Such a link would be a lifeline to me, and there are many people who owe their lives to the link established by Keston College with believers in the East.

An article about the poetess Irina Ratushinskaya drew my attention. She was serving a seven-year labour-camp sentence, and had been put away in an isolation cell for six whole months at one time. What's more, they'd shaved her hair off. On the same page, the people at Keston had put a photocopy of a rather attractive picture of Irina. She had a quiet, precise face, and a full head of curly, brown hair.

I was disturbed by this report. I had heard of these cells before. Only a few months previously a piece of paper had been smuggled out of the same women's camp in Mordovia, where Irina was being held. This slip of paper described the punishment cell. It's a very small, cramped room, with a board for a bed. The temperature never rises above eight degrees centigrade, it said, and the prisoners have to live on bread and water, with a bowl of rotten cabbage soup every other day. With my mind's eye, I could see this woman sitting there, squatting between the wall and the floor, in the cold of her cell. With her arms round her legs to try and keep warm, and with the bald obscenity of her head which had once been covered in vivacious, curly hair.

Each Tuesday a group meets in our church to pray for people in trouble. I took along the bulletin about Irina. As I read it out, a woman began to sob. I could see that Anne shared with me the sense of grief and outrage that this sort of thing could happen to one whom we felt to be our sister. Irina had already spent 138 days in punishment cells, but now for her to be put away for six months at one stretch on little more than bread and water in this chilly, draughty cell, cut us both to the quick. I think everybody else was shaken by it, but somehow it was Anne's tears that drove me to action. I knew that I had to do something, and not just go round talking about Irina. In this country we have so many words, so much information, it just flows over us, and the more we listen but can take no action, the more paralyzed we feel. In any case, what's one woman's life, when you can hear on the news of hundreds dying in an air crash? You can go and see the pieces lying all over the place and it becomes a ghoulish entertainment because it doesn't expect anything of the viewer. I felt goaded to be no longer just a viewer but to let it affect me more deeply.

At first, I didn't know quite what to do about it. I knew there had to be something visual which would illustrate Irina's plight, but I realized that the first thing to do was to find out as much as I could about her. I rang Keston and asked them to send press cuttings, poems, pictures and any other details that they could find about her. Their response was prompt and I was soon able to sit down and piece together the story.

Irina was born on 4 March 1954, in Odessa, a maritime port and seaside resort on the Black Sea coast of the Soviet Ukraine. She was of Polish stock. Her forebears were aristocrats who owned large estates in the area of Poland which was subsequently annexed by the Soviet Union. Odessa had become embroiled in the bitter fighting on the Eastern front in the Second World War. The Germans pressed east across the Ukraine, only to be halted by Russian tanks as their lines grew extended. The Soviet army pushed them back and liberated Russian prisoners of war. But then another bitterness arose: many of those Russian soldiers who had allowed themselves to be taken prisoner rather than fighting to their death were sent off to Siberia for ten or fifteen years. It was assumed they had collaborated with the Nazis. Anyone whose Soviet pedigree lay in any doubt kept very quiet in those post-war years, and Irina's parents tried to suppress any desire that their daughter might have to enquire about their Polish past.

'There was plenty to fear,' she writes, 'from officials snooping about our pedigree. Remembrance is not safe for Soviets, we Soviets!'

But Irina was not the sort to be deterred. She became intrigued to know where she had come from and the key lay largely with her ageing grandmother. A devout Catholic, the old lady often went to church, despite being pulled in by the KGB many times to try to dissuade her. Presumably it was a great embarrassment to the rest of the family who wanted to merge into the background of Soviet society.

Irina was a very bright pupil at school, but was never able to take the Soviet substitute religion seriously, in spite of being offered nothing else to take its place. She felt her Polish spirit frolicking inside her and her love of life made her dissatisfied with the half-baked Soviet philosophy which was pressed home on every occasion. Her poems feature a great-grandfather who died in action in the Civil War, fighting against the Bolsheviks. This discovery must have made

Irina realize that her family had within it an independent spirit which might raise itself again in her generation. Even as a child she loved the arts. She wrote crisp, mischievous, romantic poems. She painted water colours. She couldn't stand small rooms, corridors or lifts.

At university, she felt that if she could study the arts, which is what she really wanted to do, she would have to declare her hand. She found the official Soviet writing so drab that she knew her natural vivacity would soon land her in trouble. So she chose physics. Physics, she thought, was much the same in East or West. A communist electron is much the same as a capitalist one. And by this wise little side-step, she managed to enjoy her university years.

She had a great time. She was a very gregarious person and loved being out of doors. You could never find her in her room, according to one of her personal friends, because she was always out hiking or camping in the woods. Or else she'd be swimming from Odessa's beautiful beach. She could swim two miles offshore with no trouble, much to the anxiety of her more faint-hearted friends. At table tennis she beat her male and female opponents alike. All in all, she defied the stereotype of a poet sitting miserably in a garret, searching for metaphors. She worked her passage through university in a variety of jobs, and in 1972 angered the KGB by resisting their efforts to recruit her.

They had competitions between the departments for the wittiest student sketch, and it soon became obvious that the best scripts were written by one Irina Ratushinskaya.

She taught in a school from 1975 to 1978, at first on teaching practice, and then as a graduate teacher of gifted students. In 1977, she helped to write the script for a revue at one of the theatres in Odessa. The show was taken off after the first night because the authorities felt uneasy about it. All participants were taken in for questioning by the KGB.

It was while she was teaching at the school that somebody lent her, for a few days, the writings of poets who were not officially approved. She read, for instance, the poetry of Marina Tsvyetayeva. This woman and her family had returned voluntarily to the Soviet Union at the time of the

Second World War. Her husband went to fight at the front. Marina Tsvyetayeva was twenty-five years old at the time of the Revolution. She took up a firm anti-Bolshevik stand. Her husband, Sergei, was a White cavalry man in the Civil War and they emigrated to Prague and then to Paris when their position in Russia became untenable.

Yet they both loved their country and could not stay away. Sergei returned first and became a convinced communist. Marina followed in 1938. With the start of hostilities, Sergei fought at the front and was killed early in the war. Marina's son was exiled to one of Stalin's labour camps in the Soviet Far East, and died there, leaving his mother on her own in the world. She herself was exiled to the small provincial Russian town of Yelabuga, where she could find no means of earning a living. In her melancholy and despair, she could not even gain enough money to buy bread and chose to hang herself rather than starve to death.

Tsvyetayeva wrote poetry all the way through this bitter experience, and these were the verses that somebody lent to Irina in Odessa. Their effect on her was dramatic. 'I had them in my hands only briefly, but I devoured them. They literally threw me to my knees, physically shaking with delirium and fever. An abyss opened up before me and, unlike a normal nightmare where you can see yourself as an observer on the edge, I was thrown deep within, completely severed from whatever safe opening I'd come from. All my senses of history and literature were splintered. All my pent-up notions of who I might have been were stirred into motion. Was this the Polish spirit frolicking of its own accord now? I couldn't say. Up until now, although I could never take the Soviet religion seriously, nothing had arisen as a substitute. How could I go up into the clouds of religion-seeking when I had never had my feet on the solid ground of any homeland on earth? Clearly something for which I had not been looking had now found me! It was as if a long-forgotten God had all along been buoying me up and guarding my soul when no one had been allowed to fulfil that role in all my years of childhood and youth . . . '

This experience undoubtedly gave her life a new perspective. She described her schooling as her pseudo-education. Never had the existence of any poets even been suggested, other than the officially sanctioned ones—except to say that some poets were renegades and despicable characters to be avoided. Their works, of course, were not offered for inspection!

She coveted the years she had lost. It should have been at four or five not at twenty-four that she discovered the other world around her. It was as if she had only been taught half the alphabet. The official Soviet books were deliberately 'half-baked'.

From that moment, she vowed she would be true to the new world that she now perceived. She saw clearly that her days were numbered, that no one could write as Tsvyetayeva wrote without drawing the full wrath of the system.

'Okay, I'll do it. I'll make up those lost years. I won't lose the thread as long as I live—as long as I'm not thrown into prison or a psychiatric ward. Do I have a chance? That's a rhetorical question, dear reader.'

The new-born poet threw herself into her calling with complete vigour and inventiveness. Between that day and her arrest, she wrote 110 poems with a growing clarity. Her poetry is full of fun.

Sometimes it's fun untinged with melancholy, as in this poem about the steps by the sea in Odessa.

> And here I go flying down the steps—
> Almost in somersaults—as in a dream
> And the day is spring-like
> to the point of madness,
> And the yard with its streets is spring-like!
> And there's no salvation from the storming
> devil in me . . .
> And there's a smell of tom-cats and hops,
> From the dried flagstones
> And I pant with April
> And shout to my brother—
> 'You look miserable!'

She wrote of her dreams of flying aeroplanes and of visiting Italy, of buying a big black dog and of falling in love. She had other dreams too which she wanted to avoid—the dread of seeing friends return in twenty years from camps to which she had betrayed them.

> Not for me twenty years on
> To forget the freedom of my youth,
> Incline my grey head guiltily—
> And close the springtime window . . .
> Not for me the fate of one day meeting
> My friends with their strained voices,
> Learning the judgment passed on them—
> and being silent
> Following helplessly with my eyes
> And feeling the imprint of betrayal.

That would raise a few official eyebrows—to write of the gulag.

Irina could never settle to the official Soviet ideology, political parades were ubiquitous and well-nigh compulsory. She sought to bring them down to earth with a bump.

> How unfortunate for the parade;
> On the Palace Square—it's raining!
> The shields on the facade are streaming,
> The proletarian banner is floating
> In something sticky . . . .

She wrote a poem dedicated to that great-grandfather of hers, a Lieutenant Colonel of the Civil War, presumably not on the Bolshevik side! (A verst is approximately a kilometre.)

> Two versts from the River Dvina
> With a bullet in your throat—
> In your last agonies—
> In the middle of your war
> You threw back your arms forever . . .
> Your thunderstorm has drifted off.
> We are sunk in the shame of alien parades
> But your eyes have been given me—
> As a curse
> And as an award.

It was enough to make the authorities distinctly jumpy. I'd been in the homes of Christian families in Moscow and heard the children's quips about the gallery of Soviet leaders down the years since the Revolution. They don't translate very well but they were funny, and how can you suppress children's riddles without looking ridiculous yourself?

Irina's poetry has an impishness that no force can suppress. She is too eloquent to be silenced and the authorities never managed to silence her— neither in the court-room nor in the camp.

In 1978, she was appointed to the lecturing staff of Odessa's teacher training college. She did well and was promoted to the entrance selection board. When it was suggested to her that special entrance requirements should be applied to discriminate against Jewish applicants, she refused. Consequently, she was demoted and taken off the board although they continued to employ her as a lab assistant.

In 1979, she moved to Kiev to marry Igor Gerashchenko, who had been a friend from early childhood. He had trained as a physicist but because of his appeals to the Soviet authorities on behalf of friends, he was never able to get a job in keeping with his training.

They lived a happy but precarious life together and from all accounts were very devoted to each other. Irina was not granted a residence permit from the Kiev local authorities and this prevented her from getting a full-time teaching job. However, she gave private physics and maths tutoring to earn a living. They had to move frequently. One stay was only three weeks—a house lent to them while someone was away.

> On Batyev Hill—
> There our house stood . . .
> A three-week habitation,
> A temporary shelter.
> The wine we have not drunk
> Others will drink.
> There was nothing to lose—
> And the keys were in one's hand . . .
> But we had to say goodbye.
> Grief was no trouble!

> It was no longer hard
> For us to live—anywhere.

People ask, 'Is Irina's poetry political?' At this stage, I believe she was just holding a mirror up to the Soviet state. By bringing it down to earth, she showed what the system looked like through the eyes of one who was not and never claimed to be a worshipper of the status quo. But the 'powers that be' were not amused.

They tried twice to obtain exit visas, once to the United States and once to Israel, but were turned down. Then in August 1981, both were hauled in to the local KGB and given a dressing down. Igor was told he must stop activities in defence of others and with Irina they spelled it out very clearly: 'Either you stop writing poetry or you go to prison.' She made her decision with glaring clarity and with her pen—by continuing to write what was in her heart, as faithfully as she had ever done. It was like Daniel continuing his prayers in disregard for the king's edict, and in disregard for the den of lions which he knew was only a prayer away.

In November 1981, Igor lost even the meagre employment that he had. So in December, when they went to Moscow to mark Human Rights Day they were both out of a proper job. As an act of solidarity with Andrei Sakharov they doffed their hats in Pushkin Square.

The baptism of fire in Butyrki did not throw Irina off her stride. She was not the victim. It was she who had taken the initiative, not the state. It was the inexorable consequence of the path she had chosen and she had the stamina for it. She even got out her pen one evening and found a scrap of paper to write a poem dedicated to Igor, who was imprisoned in another place.

> Where are you my prince?
> On what plank bed?
> (No, I won't cry: I promised after all!)
> My eyes are drier than a fire
> This is only the beginning . . .
> Are you falling asleep?
> It's late.
> I'll dream of you tonight.

After the ten-day administrative sentence, they were released and returned to their precarious life in Kiev. They had to depend on casual work throughout 1982, taking odd jobs and decorating people's flats to earn enough money to survive.

In April they returned one day to the flat which, for the time being, was their home, surprising two strange men in the entrance hall. The men fled and got away in a waiting car. It turned out that they had been spraying the inside of the flat with a toxic chemical. For several days, Igor, Irina and three other people living on the same floor suffered the ill-effects—chest pains, headaches and dizziness. They reported the incident to the police, who apparently refused to investigate.

The late summer brought harvest time to the granary of Russia. There were vacancies for *shabashniki*, casual labourers, at the apple harvest in the orchards of the surrounding collective farms. Igor and Irina both joined in. They could earn as much in a few weeks picking apples as they could for the rest of the year. Payment was in kind. The workers got a load of apples which could be sold for cash at the market in Kiev. It was a bit of private enterprise that was in the broad grey area of the Soviet economy. The state depended on it but the arrangement officially did not seem to exist!

The pressure was building up on Igor and Irina by this time, and Irina started to think of the future and what lay in store for her. She writes:

> I had a strange dream last night:
> I was to be shot at dawn.
> I was imprisoned in a concrete basement
> From which the dawn was not visible.
> And then one of my class-mates appeared
> . . . somehow nobody asked me,
> They just gave me a pistol and sent me.
> You've just no idea how bad
> It makes me feel, but what can you do?

On a dry morning in September they were working together on the apple harvest at the farm. Suddenly the peace was broken. Three Volga cars loaded with plain-clothes police came roaring into the apple orchard in a cloud of dust. Under the command of a Captain Lukyamenko of the Ukrainian KGB, they burst out of the cars and approached the trees. Their target was Irina, and they soon surrounded her. The handcuffs clicked into place on her wrists. Igor was standing by. They threatened him that he would be next—and were gone. The dust settled. There were more apples to pick.

I calculate that I was finishing my breakfast with Sue and baby Christopher in our little Welsh terraced house in Bangor, where I was working as an orthopaedic and accident surgeon. It seems a long time ago. It was a Friday morning —17 September 1982.

3

SENTENCED

They drove Irina into the centre of Kiev, and swung off Vladimirskaya Street in through the gates of an old wooden building (No.33). This had been the Gestapo headquarters during the German occupation and now served as the Central KGB investigation prison for the Kiev area.

Then the work began. Eighty-three people or more in Moscow, Leningrad, Kiev and Odessa were interrogated in connection with her case. Most of them were *shabashniki* from the collective farm. Twenty-six KGB officers were involved in the Kiev operation alone. Some interrogations took as long as seventeen hours.

The investigators wanted details of any anti-Soviet comments that Irina had made. Only if these surfaced would the *shabashniki* be given their apples. Without this reward, their whole season's pay went by the board. Even so, it seems that their testimony did not agree. No real case could be put together which would stand up in court. Nobody who was interrogated was told why Irina was being charged.

Igor was arrested briefly, much to the distress of his eminent scientist father, and then released. Flats were searched in Kiev, and other antics carried out in order to find her poems. They had been typed out and then photographically reduced on to film the size of a visiting card. One page even showed a moth that had fluttered into the dark room. These little books of cards circulated widely in the Soviet Union. Even though there cannot have been many, they could nevertheless reach a huge readership, being passed around from hand to hand every few days.

Somehow Irina continued to write.

Five paces to the window and four from
wall to wall,
And the mounted eye blinks through
the iron.
The monotonous guile of the interrogation
trails past.
Oh what calmness—to wander through the
silent winter
Not even allowing the word 'No' to fall
from cracked, sewn up lips!
I am already on the road. And God's hand
is on my shoulder.

Not much was known about those months. She was allowed
no contact with the outside world, no visit from Igor nor
from her mother. No letters. But she gave as good as she
got. They could prise nothing out of her. Not a word, it
seems.

Her trial lasted three days in early March. Soviet
courts are very plain and utilitarian. The bare rough boards
of the witness box and an equally inglorious desk for the
judge. The court was open to the public, and was packed
out by workers from a nearby factory who arrived early. By
the time Irina's family arrived there was no room for them
in the gallery—or anywhere else. They were not allowed in.
The justice was as rough as the woodwork. No one who
knew Irina was called as a witness. It all depended therefore
on the bought witnesses from the apple harvest and their
purchased memories of anti-Soviet conversations, but that
fell through. The charge of anti-Soviet agitation and propaganda was made more precise, namely the manufacture
and dissemination of anti-Soviet propaganda in verse form.

Irina was forbidden an attorney of her choice. She refused the services of the state-appointed defence counsel
—who in the process of defending her admitted her guilt.
He stated that she should not be given a full sentence because her propaganda was so crude that it had led no one
else into a 'path of crime'!

Irina was denied permission to defend herself. The
charge was based on five of her poems, but had they known,
they could have included the ones she was making up as she

sat in the dock. The judges returned, perhaps after lunch:

> And it's turned out to be simply boring—
> No more than that. The cramped space
> Of the cell, the enclosure of the stuffy
> court-room.
> Eye to Eye! A childish triumph!
> They're coming back! Are they afraid of
> uproar in the court?
> Does my cheerful gaze seem fierce,
> Like a convict's? Do they dream I'll get
> them by the throat?
> But my brigandage has already been
> overcome
> By the pride my forefathers chiselled out:
> What had these servile eyes to do with me?

For her final statement she chose to recite to the court:

> My hateful Motherland!
> There is nothing more shameful than your
> nights!
> How lucky you were
> With your holy fools!
> Your serfs and executioners!
> How good you were at spawning loyal
> subjects . . .

The judge cut her short. They couldn't stand it any longer, nor could they silence her, except by refusing to listen.

The scene reminds one of the trial of Stephen, the first Christian martyr.

'And gazing at him, all who sat in the council saw that his face was like the face of an angel . . . Now when they heard these things they were enraged, and they ground their teeth against him . . . they cried out with a loud voice and stopped their ears and rushed together upon him . . . they cast him out of the city and stoned him.'

You'll have to judge for yourself whether or not her poetry is political. It surely laments and rebukes a system which 'zealously destroys all those who could not be bought or sold.' Irina was not to be bought or sold and went to serve a full sentence still with an unquenchable spirit and a sparkle in her eye.

She was given seven years in a strict-regime camp, followed by exile for five years in a remote village. She and Igor could only be reunited there at the risk of losing their residence permit for Kiev and being condemned to wander the villages of Siberia for the rest of their days. Irina was the first woman to be given the maximum sentence for anti-Soviet agitation since the days of Stalin. Not only so. The then First Secretary, Andropov, introduced another law permitting labour camp authorities to extend sentences by up to five years off their own bat, for alleged breaches of camp discipline. This, Andropov decreed, could include the most minor offences such as having a shirt button undone! And the sentence could be repeated as often as necessary, without even taking the prisoner to court. The decree was not used immediately. It was under Mr Gorbachev that this move towards perpetual imprisonment was first put into effect.

Whilst in the cells awaiting confirmation of her sentence, Irina developed toothache.

> That traitress and apostate,
> That mote in the government's eye,
> That especially dangerous criminal—
> What a joke!—she's cutting a tooth.
> My good for nothing wisdom!
> You've chosen a fine place to assert your
> rights!
> The regulations forbid possession
> Of this sharp cutting object!
> 'What do you mean, it just *grew*? That's
> impossible!'

At an appeal, the verdict and sentence were upheld. She was sent off to the camp, tooth and all. They didn't even give her the usual legal document confirming her verdict and sentence. Irina turned up a few weeks later in Barashevo, Mordovia some 300 miles south-east of Moscow on the railway line to Saransk—by Russian calculations, not far from the Volga.

One researcher, an ex-prisoner, reported that the camp at Barashevo has a special section for women with children. The Mordovian camp complex is huge, about forty miles across, with some nineteen camps. Each camp has an estimated population of some 2,000 prisoners. The camp complex, therefore, has a population of some 38,000 souls, living under these awful conditions. So it has the same population as some British cities, for instance: Canterbury or Salisbury in the south; or in the north, Scarborough or Durham, or again, Inverness or Merthyr Tydfil. It has accommodation for warders and schools for their children. The 'capital' is at Yavas, where punishment cells and a hospital are located, and prisoners are often moved around by the camp's own railway network.

If you know where to look for them, you can find places like this all over the Soviet Union, from the islands in the Arctic Ocean to the Pacific Coast and to the borders of Afghanistan, and starting at the Lubyanka, within half a mile of Red Square.

The railway line to the camp runs from Moscow via the town of Potma. Looking out of the window you can see the bare wooden stakes which mark the graves of the prisoners who perished while they were constructing the line.

Irina arrived at the camp in April 1983 and was put with the other dozen or so women political and religious prisoners in the 'small zone', a separate compound away from the criminals. The authorities tidied up the situation by putting all their bad eggs in one basket.

During the summer of 1983, predictably, the women in the 'small zone' became rather difficult to control.

Podust, the female section chief, was the head warder for the zone. For over a year an order had been given that politicals should wear an identity patch like criminals. This was called a *birka*. The women refused to wear it. It was a degradation in their eyes, a loss of personality. They pointed out that even the Soviets had said as much when the Nazis made the Russian POWs wear a similar patch.

Podust put her foot down. No visits from relatives and no purchases from the camp shop till they wore the *birka*.

She also insisted that the women called her 'citizen superintendent' and confiscated any more than two sets of underwear per person. 'Anyway, how are you going to have children after a spell in solitary', she leered.

The August date of Irina's visit from Igor came and went. He was expected between the eighth and the tenth. Irina's visiting rights were suspended on the ninth, but kindly restored on the twelfth.

The *birka* issue met with no resolution and the pent-up frustration of Podust erupted. A flower bed had somehow mysteriously appeared in the compound and been winked at by the guards. Even some of the flowers looked a bit nutritious, such as the green peppers! Podust brought a detachment of criminal prisoners to root up the plants. The prisoners showed some reluctance as did apparently even some of the guards. At this point Podust flew into a rage and laid into the task, flinging the uprooted plants all over the place. The debris was cleared up. The kitchens served a soup made with some beetroot tops and that was that.

On 17 August two of the other women, Tatyana and Natalya, were put in solitary for not working and not wearing the *birka*. Natalya was ill at the time, so Irina and all the others went on a hunger strike in protest. In the punishment cells where these women were confined, they had to strip and were allowed only thin prison dresses with no warm underwear, just a cotton slip. No headdress was allowed, and only short socks could be worn. Slippers were not disinfected after the previous prisoner had worn them, so fungal foot infections spread rapidly among the 2,000 strong camp population.

On the seventh day of the hunger strike they took Irina away to force-feed her. Six men handcuffed her, and in the struggle her head was banged against the head of the bed. As a result, she lost consciousness during which time they poured feeding liquid down her throat, without taking any steps to prevent her breathing it into her lungs. Another of the women, called Raisa, was not strong enough to resist; faced with the six men, she drank the liquid. The guards told the others that Raisa had co-operated, whereupon she denied it and vowed that from then on she would resist all attempts to make her compromise. The challenge soon came and they had to force her, although this time they chocked her mouth open and forced the liquid down through a stomach tube. Then they put her in a cell and the warders were told to deny her water for twenty-four hours. She pleaded for water, but in vain.

They did not put Irina in the punishment cell this time. Instead, she was transferred to a closed psychiatric isolation room, without windows or ventilation, in the hospital with one of the other prisoners. Her companion revived her. She was still suffering from nausea, dizziness and headaches five days later when they let her out.

Tatyana and Natalya were released a day early. The other women stopped the hunger-strike with the threat that they would do it again if any sick prisoner were put in the punishment cell.

Back in the 'small zone', they were still hungry. The garden plants, some of which had been edible, had been dug up. The only food was a soup made of rotten cabbage, and other bits of unsavoury stuff rejected from the warders' kitchens. It was so salty that it was practically inedible. Many of them developed pain in the loins from the cold, which was probably a kidney infection.

Some time in September, Igor came back. Although he was once more turned away, Irina discovered that he was there and went on another hunger-strike. On the third day he was allowed in to see her for a few hours, though probably unable to touch her and with a guard present. It was the last they saw of each other for three years, despite his making many more journeys all the way from Kiev some thousand miles or so via Moscow. Each time he was turned away at the gate, though he kept coming. It must have cost him dearly both in money and in sorrow.

Irina was more concerned for him than for herself. She, who could not stand small rooms and couped-up spaces, fretted for Igor in their 'cubby-hole apartment' and feared lest he be driven mad. The letters were few, said nothing and would repeatedly go astray. Rarely did she have any rights to receive parcels. And there were the regulations which excluded from parcels anything of real value to a prisoner.

According to a diary which was written and somehow smuggled out of the camp, in September the women declared an eight-day hunger-strike to mark the opening of the Madrid review conference of the Helsinki Accords. The Soviet and Western delegations were meeting, presumably in plush surroundings in the Spanish capital, but what could they do? No doubt the British produced a list of names. It would have been a gentlemanly exchange! The Soviets would have noted the names, pointed to British and American excesses and that would be that. What more could be done? But such occasions would not go unmarked in the Barashevo camp.

The authorities sent a man from Moscow to investigate the 'small-zone' problems. It was obvious to him that he wouldn't get anywhere with these women. The diary records that 'he just sniffed and went back to Moscow'. After that, the Main Directorate of Corrective Labour Institutions sent a Commission. The soup was made less salty in honour of their arrival, and the vegetables less rotten. Podust was quiet and unnaturally restrained. The visitors came and went. The soup became salty again, the vegetables rotted and Podust's blood pressure started to rise once more. The Camp Director, Pavlov, admitted within earshot that they didn't know what to do with the women.

Podust started to shout. Natalya became the butt of most of the abuse. She had been diagnosed as having appendicitis. Podust threatened the punishment cell and said sarcastically, 'How will your appendicitis recover after that?' She took every opportunity to humiliate Irina. The prisoners all agreed (with the exception of one who appeared to be an informer), not to speak to Podust and not to listen to her. Within a few days, they noticed that when Podust approached the barracks, she would hesitate and go off elsewhere, hanging around the perimeter fence, not knowing what to do. As time passed, Podust rarely appeared and gave her orders through someone else.

In November, Natalya and another woman prisoner were told to report for 'relocation'. The women didn't like the sound of that. She was ill with a temperature and pains in her stomach and chest. She needed to go to hospital but the guards said that the hospital was full. They overlooked the fact that another 'small-zone' woman was there at the time, and when she returned to the camp, she exposed the truth. There were in fact spaces in the hospital all along.

The guards said they'd take her temperature, and if it was up, then 'of course' they would not take her away. It was indeed up and they left her.

The next day they came again. The doctor took her temperature. It was still a little up. She went away, but in a few minutes the superintendent arrived, along with a Major, a Colonel and some guards. Irina and Tatyana blocked the way to Natalya's bunk, but were outnumbered and forced away. Natalya was dragged off barefoot, dressed only in her blouse and pants, out into the frost. They said they were taking her for 're-education' at the KGB investigation unit at Saransk. She screamed and called for help but they beat her up. She lost consciousness on the way but remembers the Assistant Colony Director, Shalin, kicking her with his boots.

Irina declared that she and the other women prisoners would do all they could to alert the world to Natalya's fate. Remarkably, they did manage to get word out of the camp and the incident was published in the West in November. A month later, Irina was put in the punishment cells for twelve days for striking, presumably in support of Natalya. She returned to the zone on 19 December, only to declare a hunger-strike until Natalya was released and given medical help. Many others joined her and the rest declared a work-strike. Irina became weak and did not work. They had to produce seventy pairs of industrial gloves each day. For not working, she was put back in solitary on 23 December into the same cell as Natalya. It was very cold.

The doctor came, diagnosed cardiac insufficiency and ordered a urine test. Natalya spent the next few days lying on the floor in severe abdominal pain, repeatedly asking for help and receiving none. She lay by the radiator which was occasionally lukewarm. Irina continued to call for help. The nurse came and did the urine test. It was 'fine' and no treatment was forthcoming.

The nights were the worst. On the twenty-seventh she

41

had two 'heart attacks', wheezing and gasping. The nurse came to the hatch and said that since the urine analysis had been so good, she would be getting no treatment. Two more attacks and she was writhing in pain. On 2 January they came in and carried her out. Irina told them she would continue to fast until she personally saw that they had admitted Natalya to hospital. On 4 January Irina saw Natalya's figure through a window in the hospital and ended her hunger-strike on its fifteenth day.

Clearly, the spirit of solidarity amongst the women in the camp was largely generated by Irina's unquenchable spirit, which the Kiev judge had feared so much.

They flew Raisa to Kiev for treatment in the infirmary —a stay which included several visits to the 'administrative' department of the Vladimir Skaya Street Prison for a 'chat'.

'Is Ratushinskaya cock of the roost nowadays?'

'Why is Ratushinskaya so vicious?'

Raisa was not prepared to sign an agreement and on the verge of freedom left once more for the 'small-zone', arriving back in March 1984.

During her stay, until August 1985, Irina spent at least 138 days in punishment cells. She took part in all the strikes that happened over many hundreds of days, and saw each one through.

The prisoners managed to record these events in a diary on tissue-thin bits of paper which were rolled tight and slipped out of the camp unnoticed, directed to the West.

These women were indeed a headache to the authorities charged with their control. All hell broke loose when they tried to put an elderly sick Lithuanian lady in the punishment block for ten days. Irina was in the punishment block at the time, but as soon as she returned she declared another hunger-strike to last till Jadvyga returned safely. In fact the old lady survived pretty well. The others managed to get some extra clothes on to her before she was taken away and for some reason, the guards did not check that she'd been properly stripped and dressed in punishmentcell rags. But she did come back with heart and kidney pains.

Then again, while Irina was sent away to hospital at the camp HQ, the authorities put Tatyana and Natalya in

42

solitary again for not working. The guards found that they were both wearing sweat shirts. The chief of the regulations section ordered that they be confiscated immediately, as well as their slippers and socks. They refused. Then they threatened to handcuff the pair and undress them by force. At this point Natalya removed all her clothes and set off back to the cell naked, whereupon the guards rushed after her and persuaded her to put her clothes on again!

The diary finishes with the intriguing comment that Podust was summoned to Moscow, promoted and transferred to another camp. 'She is winding up her work here,' the diarist continues, 'waiting for her children to finish the school year. The administration insist that Podust's transfer is in no way connected with our demand for her removal.' Of course not!

Igor continued his long, faithful vigil, traipsing back and forth to the camp. He went to the Kiev KGB to demand a visit. Denial gave way to consent, but only to a short visit which was thereafter cancelled for some supposed misdemeanour.

Irina says she'll go on striking till she sees Igor. Fellow prisoners express concern for her survival. Igor appeals to 'All Western Parliamentarians':

'Dear Sirs,
I appeal to all those in whose hearts courage has not been replaced by cowardice or indifference. Help me to save my wife in the name of the woman who gave you birth or the woman you love. The greatest fear for man is indifference and cowardice. Indifference makes it possible for the most terrible crimes to happen. Irina's terrible fate is real now in the USSR, but with silent consent it could happen also to your wife and daughter in your, so far, democratic country. Think about that, when you come home and look into the eyes of your loved ones.'

Obscurity draws a veil over the next eighteen months, but in August 1985 things seemed to hot up again. On 7 August Irina was taken to the punishment cells at Yavas, some ten to fifteen miles away, by road. The reason for this is not clear. The vehicle was a kind of 'black maria', well known in the prison service, where they call it a 'Raven' (*Voronok*). It was unsprung and had two tiny cells for specially dangerous prisoners, such as the politicals, as well as a more general area for others. All prisoners were transported by being crammed into these vehicles, sitting on benches and squatting on the floor. Apart from the cells, the back of a 'Raven' measures about five feet square. Amnesty International reports one witness who saw twenty-five women prisoners, one with a child, unloaded from a 'Raven' in the Mordovian camp complex. In April 1979, in Kazan on the Volga, seventeen prisoners died of suffocation in a 'Raven' which had been left standing in the sun without anyone answering the prisoners' repeated cries to be let out.

Irina went to Yavas. On the way the vehicle hit a rut. As a result, she was bounced around in the back, hit her head and suffered concussion. A doctor saw her and confirmed that she was concussed. On the same day she was beaten unconscious by three female warders and a male warder, stripped to her underwear, and dragged along the corridor to be dumped on the stone floor outside the punishment cell. Later, some prisoners carried her into the cell. She had to lie on the cold stone floor of the unheated cell all week.

After seven days she was taken back to the camp. The local doctor, a psychiatrist and a neurologist all saw her—a pretty impressive turn-out for rural Mordovia. Once more they confirmed concussion. She was excused work and continued with some medication which had been started at Yavas. When the doctors had gone, however, and Irina started bringing legal proceedings against her assailants, she was immediately sent off again to the camp prison for five months for 'pretending that she had concussion'.

On 30 August, she went on hunger-strike again because the cell was unheated and the temperature never rose above twelve degrees centigrade, very cold for any prolonged period. It was the *Keston News* report of this session in the camp prison which first drew my attention. They got it more or less right, though it was turned out to be a five-month camp sentence, not six.

I must admit to being both horrified and intrigued by the whole set-up. How can you survive the gnawing cold? How can the guards keep up the aggression when they presumably would rather be in Moscow or Kiev, too? How does Podust get on with her kids when they come home from school and expect their mum to make their tea? Who is this Podust? Has she a husband, and does she bottle beetroot?

And Ratushinskaya—is she a bitch or an angel? Is it all another world or are these people like us?

> I will live and survive and be asked
> How they slammed my head against
> a trestle,
> How I had to freeze at nights,
> How my hair started to turn grey . . .
> But I'll smile. And will crack some joke
> And brush away the encroaching shadow.

Yet Irina's survival was in doubt, at any rate amongst her friends, as another smuggled slip of paper revealed:

'We women political prisoners wish to tell you of our friend Irina Ratushinskaya. Her fate deserves the special attention of the world, and her fate depends directly on this attention. Irina is a talented poetess. She is a person of lively and precise mind, a courageous and hard-working human rights activist. Intelligence, talent and fearlessness—this combination was considered by the KGB to be particularly dangerous. She came to the camp healthy, but for many months now, Irina has been a sick woman. Despite her illness, more than once she has declared a strike or fast in defence of others and this leads to further punishment for her. Irina still has more than five years of her camp sentence to serve, and if they are the same as the first years then she simply will not live to the end.'

4

I MUST DO SOMETHING

Irina's need was urgent, and I felt I couldn't let another day pass without trying to do something to help her. But what?

I got in the car and headed off to the BBC Studios at Pebble Mill. The modern studios face on to a pleasant treelined avenue—a dual carriageway, with comfortable detached houses opposite. I kicked around in the fallen leaves and suddenly it came to me. The cameras sometimes look out of the large studio windows across the road. 'How about putting a cage in one of the front gardens opposite, and live in it for a few weeks? They'd see it every day coming to work and would surely send someone out to interview me.'

This brilliant idea had only one immediate flaw. I'd have to get permission from the owner of one of the houses. I hesitated on the pavement before going to ring the doorbell. What would I say?

'Good morning, I'm a clergyman. I know I may not look like it in my jeans, but I am, and I'm worried about a woman in prison in Russia. Please may I live in a cage in your garden for a fortnight?'

No problem. I advanced a step or two towards the door of one of the larger houses, but then it occurred to me that only the wife would be at home in the daytime. She would want to discuss it with her husband on his return. You can just imagine it, can't you. 'Oh darling, did you have a good day at the office? There's been a man here who wants to live in a cage in our garden.' It suddenly became a lot less persuasive when I thought how it would sound second-hand. I faltered. It also occurred to me that, of course, the BBC might possibly resent a chap coming and putting up a demo right in front of their windows. If I rubbed them up the wrong way, it wasn't likely that Central TV would be keen to come and cover a story which had been so obviously designed for use by its competitor.

I drove into town and wandered around looking for other likely places. The churchyard of Birmingham Cathedral seemed an excellent place. There were lots of people around and with Christmas shopping coming up, there would be lots more. It was church land so I wouldn't have to go and convince the city council, just the Provost of the Cathedral and presumably he would understand these things. I wanted to put up a cage in the churchyard, with a tarpaulin as a roof, and live in it with nothing to eat for two weeks leading up to Christmas. It would make the shoppers think as they went home, laden with opulent goodies. They'd think of this poor woman stagnating in her cell in the freezing cold. But how about the cage? What if it snowed or poured with rain for several days? I could use a big tarpaulin and let part of it down as a wall against the weather.

With these thoughts in my mind I entered the Cathedral and climbed the stairs to the office. I asked to see the Provost.

'I'm sorry, there isn't one!' the secretary replied. 'The last one left a few weeks back and the next one hasn't arrived yet.'

Any application had to be made in writing to the Senior Residentiary Canon. I couldn't reach him on the phone, so I had to go home to compose my letter. It didn't come out well at first and eventually, it took me four long pages to explain the position as persuasively as I could. I delivered the letter by hand to the office to save time, both for Irina and in order to get the show on the road before Christmas.

I rang the next day. The Residentiary Canon had been.

'Did he see my letter?'

'Oh yes—he did. He saw your letter all right!'

I wasn't very reassured at the way the secretary put it!

There was no reply for several days, so I rang again the next week. In the absence of a provost my request had been referred to the Bishop. That worried me a bit. It was one thing to present your ideas to a provost, but quite another to muck up any possible career in the Church of England by parading your loony ideas in front of a bishop. I tried to get to the Bishop before my letter did, but it was too late. He was not to be persuaded. There were all sorts of reasons why he could not let me do it. I must admit that they didn't seem very cogent at the time, but in the long run, as you will see, I'm glad he did say no.

I felt a bit bruised but I couldn't let it rest there. Irina was still stagnating in her cell. I tried out the idea of a pedestrian area in Colmore Circus, near the city centre, but the police weren't keen on that idea. Then, after endless negotiations with a city councillor and a horticultural adviser, it was agreed I could use a park near Pebble Mill.

I'd been hunting around for nearly a month by this time and all I had was this not very promising opening. I couldn't do anything public before Christmas. All this time Irina, was in her cell and I felt anguish that the time was going by and she was still sitting it out. So on the day when I should have started my time in the cage, I started a private fast at home for five days. My five-year-old son, Christopher, didn't seem to be a bit bothered that his Dad had only a glass of water for breakfast and again for tea, only a little curious.

To test the whole idea out, I went to see Father David Hutt. He was the vicar at a church not far from the city centre, although it was not close enough to be any use as a place for the cage. I had a great respect for him and I knew of his concern for prisoners suffering in Russia. As I went to see him, on the first day of my fast, I knew we would be on the same wavelength.

I retold the story and asked him if he thought the whole idea was mad.

'No, I don't!' he said. 'I think it's got mileage in it. It will be very effective, but to maximize the effect you need—I hardly dare say the word —a committee! You need a chairman, maybe yourself, a treasurer, a secretary, a stage manager and someone to look after the public relations. You could do it here if you wanted to, but it's a bit out of the way. I'd join your committee, but I'm just moving to a church in London!'

I discussed the timing of it and we agreed that now, given the delay, I should cut my losses and 'go for Lent'. It was a great relief to have talked to someone else about it all, and to have had some positive come-back.

Mark Taylor, a good friend and a doctor at the Children's Hospital, agreed to be chairman. I knew he'd do a good job. We had worked together before. He wasn't impressed with the idea of the park. He thought it would have all the wrong appearances and I would be easily interpreted as a nutter.

'You really need a church,' he said. 'To have it in a church

48

gives it the church's moral backing and stops it being seen as just a cranky individual idea.'

Mark agreed to keep an eye on me medically too.

One woman, whom I had heard of in theatrical design, gave me some good tips.

'Be smart, use a metal scaffolding frame so that it doesn't all collapse on you half-way through, and make it a bit bigger than you need. It will be more eye-catching.'

Another friend, George Buckley, had time on his hands after being made redundant from a senior management job at Cadbury's. He had been through a pretty tough time and had become rather depressed and frustrated. I asked him if he'd be treasurer. He'd been used to shipping container loads of chocolate all over the world, ensuring that they would not melt on the dock-side in some tropical port, so I figured he must be a capable administrator. He took the job.

Michael Bojarowski, also a trusted friend, runs a small engineering works in Smethwick. His niece has been under a suspended sentence in the Soviet Union over the last few years for her activities as a Christian. Whatever happened, I wanted Michael's support. He knew first hand about the situation facing believers in the Eastern Bloc and I could trust him.

What about someone to deal with the press and manage the public relations? No one sprang to mind. I rang Michael Blood, a local vicar who does religious broadcasting for BBC Radio West Midlands. He'd already helped me a lot and I thought he'd have some good ideas. He sounded interested. To him, this was no more unusual than a Baptist minister he had featured on his programme once, who had run away to join a circus! He encouraged me to get in touch with a friendly PR consultant in Halesowen called Nick Mendes.

I drove over to Halesowen and kept an appointment to see the boss of registered Public Relations Consultants, Mendes and Associates. It was a bright December morning. The sun streamed into the plush office as I sat at the large conference table with this impressive man. He listened to me, endorsed the plans completely, then came straight to the point.

'Irina's had her hair shaved off, you say. Why don't you too?' I'd been thinking of it but felt it might be seen as a bit 'over the top'.

'It would have great visual impact, and once it's off, don't shave. Let people see your hair grow. It's a sign of how long you've been there. Dress smartly. Get glamorous people there to support you,' he advised.

He wasn't able to spend time on it himself, but he went through the directory of the Institute of Public Relations, writing out a list of all the retired members or fellows who he thought might have something to offer: a British officer in charge of secret operations in wartime France, an admiral, and retired PR consultants who had been in government, the chain stores, the Salvation Army and hosts of others.

Christmas crept up on us and afterwards Sue, Christopher and I drove to London to stay with my parents. While I was there, I decided to chase up a few PR people for the committee. My parents must have realized something was afoot, hearing snatches of conversation about cages and having my hair shaved off. I told them our plans. Poor Mum and Dad! I think they had grown to expect me to do some rather outrageous things. Apart from being worried that I'd be written off as a crank, they bore it well.

I got through to some of the PR people. Jeanne Townsend, who handled the campaign to help the Boat People after the evacuation from Saigon, was very helpful. She wrote screeds of notes, giving tips about how to communicate with the press. She felt very strongly that it should be a crusade by *local* people for Irina; ordinary people doing things well—but it shouldn't be too slick.

'Make sure you log every call,' she said, 'so you know which journalist you've got through to and can contact them again when necessary. On your press release, include a phone number and then be sure that phone is operated all the time by someone who knows what's going on. Produce a professional display made, if possible, by an exhibition company. Display the press cuttings as they build up. You will need an office manager.' Perhaps most importantly she said, 'You don't need to be too modest. Don't worry if the limelight falls on you for the time being. You're well able to deflect it where you want to, namely, on Irina!'

The ex-vicar of Fleet Street's parish church couldn't pull any strings for me, as he had been a confidential pastor to the newspaper barons, and couldn't betray their trust by misusing this position. But he also gave me some very good tips.

'Make up a press list out of a press directory such as *Willings*,' he suggested. 'It has all the addresses and phone numbers you'll need. Hold a press conference and have plenty of spare hand-outs for those who will have left their press release behind. At the press conference, don't serve drinks or offer other enticements. People will only ask who's paying for it, and become suspicious. You've a story to tell and it will sell itself, so you don't need to resort to such tactics.'

In London I met Peter Thompson, an expert in Parliamentary lobbying. In the mid 70s he had worked for the release of some innocent teenagers who were serving long sentences in Turkish jails. The then Foreign Secretary and Lord Chancellor had helped him and his experience in this regard was invaluable. He was not sure about the value of the proposed fast and the involvement of the media. He stressed that it was lobbying of the Government that would win the day. Looking back I can see his wisdom . . . He also told me to find out who else in Britain and other countries was working for her release, and to contact them.

'I'm not suggesting an international conference,' he said, 'but you ought to find out what they are up to.'

I had to admit he had a point. Within a week of his probing, I had linked up with people in many countries. The Norwegians and Swedes already had their governments involved. The Russian emigre community in Paris had published a lot about her and various missions and human-rights groups had taken up her case very vigorously. The international league of writers, the 'PEN Club' (Poets, Essayists and Novelists), had passed a motion at a recent world congress in New York, in which they called for Irina's release. The Bukovsky Foundation in Amsterdam had published a lot of her writings and were working for her in a very efficient way. School children at Smoky Hills High School in Denver, Colorado had held a birthday party for her in her absence. People were ready to help in Melbourne, Australia and in Christchurch, New Zealand. That's not even mentioning the many people and groups working for her in Britain and the fact that a book of her poetry was about to be published by Bloodaxe Books in Newcastle-on-

Tyne. Best of all, I discovered a long-standing personal friend of Irina's who was keeping in constant touch with Igor by letter and on the phone as often as the censors allowed. I rang him at his home on the outskirts of Chicago, staying up into the middle of the night to do so.

So I am indebted to Mr Thompson for his blunt remarks!

None of the PR people was eventually able to join us, although each gave useful advice.

I called on Mr Max Harrison, a respected senior orthopaedic surgeon in Birmingham. I had been his assistant briefly at the Orthopaedic Hospital. I knew he felt deeply about these things. As I mentioned my plans, he became one of my best-ever advisers, helping out in many a sticky moment. He was able to open the way for some excellent support from the Jewish community and introduced me to his rabbi and to some campaigners for Soviet Jewry who had been learning the ropes for ten years or more. All this proved to be a great encouragement. He was also particularly keen for me to get the Muslims in on the campaign. I found this pretty staggering in view of the traditional antipathy between these two communities worldwide. I had known a Muslim poet and writer, Mr Mohammed Khan Qazi, and had a standing invitation to visit his home. He joined in too.

The committee met at the beginning of January in my house. We couldn't do much until we had a proper place for the cage but at least the committee could knock my plans into shape a bit. They weren't happy about the park. It had to be under cover and preferably a church. They wouldn't let me fast completely. They thought it would look a bit too much like self-immolation. I was advised to eat a bit, say bread and water, in order to re-enact Irina's conditions as much as possible. This was an important step forward and from it followed the idea of making the cage into a replica of Irina's cell in the prison. A board would act as the bed. The size of the cell was little more than the length of a bed. Like Irina, I would have only one thin blanket and the diet could be reproduced more or less as Irina's, 450 grams of bread and water and a bowl of porridge on alternate days without milk or sugar.

It sounded a bit cushy, but I took their point that I'd be more likely to remain mentally balanced on this diet than on nothing. Having decided I would eat a bit it then became possible to think of doing it, not for fourteen or twenty-five days as I had originally thought, but for the whole of Lent. I always thought Lent was forty days and forty nights but it turns out to be forty-six days. So forty-six days it was—if only we could persuade someone to let us in.

The next job, as always, was to get out and foot-slog again. I wore out a pair of shoes until we agreed that really the best place would be St Martin's in the Bull Ring. It was very central, with crowds outside milling around in the markets. I looked round. It's an old church, but most of what you see is Gothic and blackened by the industrial grime that covered everything in the industrial heart of the Midlands. I entered it by the main door, through the draught-excluding porch. It was like entering a cathedral—very dark inside, but warm, and with someone behind the desk to welcome visitors. I tried to remain anonymous as I had a look round inside the back of the church. The ideal site was either in a vacant area at the back of the church in the foot of the tower, where there stood a life-size crib (which would have done, almost unaltered).

However, I knew there was a problem. They had no rector. The church was in a gap between rectors, with Ray Price, the Markets Chaplain in charge, who could not decide for the new man who was coming in February. Knowing that Lent started on 12 February and that I'd have to start then in order to get off on a good footing, I asked when he would be able to make a decision. No one knew.

I'd never met the new rector of course, and sympathetic as Ray Price was to the idea, he couldn't predict either. It all felt terribly nebulous. What rector arriving to make his mark on the city would start by having a man in a cell in his church in the first fortnight of his ministry there? It seemed unlikely that a decision would be made in time to use St Martin's, much to my regret.

I worked systematically through all the churches in the city centre that seemed anywhere near the right kind of venue. Nothing turned up. I must admit that I became a bit frustrated. The pattern became familiar. I began to feel like a gramophone record which was stuck in a groove.

'I'm an Anglican clergyman and an orthopaedic surgeon as well.'

'Oh yes.'

'And I'm concerned about a woman in a Russian labour camp on bread and water who is in a freezing cold cell with her head shaved . . .'

I soon got the hang of the reply too. People were all very concerned and wanted to help, but when they thought about it, there would be problems. Some said it was an heroic gesture but nevertheless, 'We'd have to have it cleared out for weddings, or it would be distracting for the atmosphere of worship, or where would the choir boys relax after choir practice?'

Some felt it was too political and, although they felt for Irina, they also thought it might damage their quiet negotiations with the Soviets. I've never seen it that way myself. I got used to these responses.

'A great idea, but I foresee problems.'

On hearing of the meagre clothing allowed in punishment cells, one church leader groaned, 'Urgh! You're not going to sit there in your underpants are you?' End of discussion!

I felt a bit cheesed off with the church and its desire for propriety in the face of the opportunity to help Irina. I paced the city streets looking for empty shops. I felt the pathos of it. I could almost hear the violins! A trendy-looking boutique was closing down and I asked when it was opening up again. The only answer would come from a development company in London who didn't sound promising. There was a prime-site shop complex lying empty not far from the site I'd considered originally at Colmore Circus, and others scattered around the central shopping area. Each was fraught with problems. Of course, the estate agents wanted to let them out to proper commercial clients. There was no way I could afford to rent them or even pay the rates, but at least if they stayed technically unoccupied, they would be unlikely to be charged rates. To satisfy that requirement, they probably need to have no electricity supply. Without lights, probably nobody would have noticed the cage. Undoubtedly, it would have looked wrong, but in the absence of any church, perhaps it would have to do.

The plush estate agents' commercial offices gave me a sympathetic hearing but no one came up with any firm offers of a place.

Then I tried the shopping centres. They would be really

great, under cover and protected by the security men, taking the whole campaign 'to the people'.

However, the first shopping-centre manager was quite blunt. He was sorry for Irina but it would be dishonest of him, he said, to raise my hopes. It wasn't on. The next was more hopeful. They had nearly done something in this vein before in the human-rights field. The manager gave me an appointment to see him, but on the day he ended up in bed with the flu. His letter a few days later apologized and said that the demonstration was of a political nature, and as such unsuitable for a shopping centre. He didn't want to upset the tenants.

'I would suggest somewhere like a church,' he said. This last sentence hit home particularly hard after all my rejections.

I began to panic. Time was nearly running out, and there was no place to put the cage. I looked longingly at the city centre pedestrian areas but these were no-go areas for me now.

A central police station controls the Bull Ring area. Outside St Martin's, in the middle of a roundabout, is a convenient alcove off a little park. The Digbeth Police seemed less apprehensive about that, so I thought I'd try it out for a night or two. Sue dissuaded me, told me to stop panicking and to wait for the committee meeting on 20 January.

I didn't want to wait. If I couldn't try out the Bull Ring, I'd keep trying less 'prime-site' religious buildings. A little West Indian Pentecostal church on the outskirts couldn't decide as their pastor was away in America. I even asked about the synagogue and the mosque. If nothing else had worked, they might have taken me. I reflected on the embarrassment this would be to the church if the only place that would have me turned out to be the mosque. I began rather to enjoy the idea.

20 January came and the committee reconvened. There was nothing to discuss. In the absence of a place to do it, the whole business looked as if it might all fade away. At least we decided on a name for ourselves. We didn't want it to sound too belligerent. It must include Irina's name and include some reference to the spiritual dimension. We wondered about 'Courage in the Gulag' or 'Guts in the Gulag' but eventually settled on 'The Irina Vigil'. The word 'vigil' seemed to denote a serious act of solidarity rather than a protest, and we didn't

want the venture to be seen primarily as a protest. So 'Irina Vigil' it was.

Mark and Mr Harrison told me to stop fretting. St Martin's was the obvious place even if it did mean waiting anxiously. Also, if I had a lot of irons in the fire when I eventually did go to see the new rector, he might feel less inclined to grant our request, thinking we'd get somewhere else eventually.

So I tried to simmer down. I went to see Ray Price, the deputy at St Martin's, and he agreed to ring and discuss it with the new rector, John Wesson.

I couldn't do anything but wait. It was tantalizing. I went down to London to meet Jamie Bogle, who'd done a spell on the tanks in the Berlin Garrison and was now a research assistant in the House of Commons. He and his journalist wife, Joanna, had become old hands at demos outside the Soviet Embassy on Irina's behalf. He gave me all sorts of tips about how to get things to the attention of the House. He said he'd get an 'Early Day Motion' put down in the House, a sort of petition by back-bench MPs to the government. What he meant was that he would approach Nicholas Winterton, the MP for Macclesfield, who was happy to 'put down' the motion. This was a great help in getting the ball rolling. It would appear on the order paper of the House of Commons every day until the end of the parliamentary session in the summer.

Amnesty International in London had some remarkable photos actually taken inside the camp which I was allowed to use to make a display. One shot showed the watch-tower on the corner of Irina's compound at the 'small zone' of the camp, which is occupied by the women political prisoners. A sturdy high wooden fence is clearly visible, topped by barbed wire and encircled by further layers of stakes with barbed wire. Another shot shows a crooked view up the gap between two perimeter fences partly obscured by the photographer's coat, draped across the lens for camouflage. A high mesh fence of tangled coils of barbed wire and a trip wire loom over a railway line on one photograph and others show the rugged camp gates, and the notice-board at the entrance to the camp displaying the rules. One picture of a barrack block even has a column of prisoners marching past it.

Back in Birmingham, John Wesson had arrived. Mark

and I put our heads together to draft a letter to him. I thought it would sound more plausible if it came from two of us, especially as Mark was a medical consultant. Mr Harrison and Mr Qazi said we could include their names. We spelt out the plans as fully as we could and made arrangements to see him.

We arrived separately at his suburban rectory. I got there first. Mr Wesson opened the door and ushered me into the living room. A fire was glowing in the grate as I sat on an elegant sofa. I made polite conversation about their move from Bristol and chatted as if I hadn't a care in the world. The sweat in my armpits wasn't because of the fire. The slight tremor wasn't from the coldness of the night.

Mark arrived, his old VW minibus popping up the road to the front door. I hoped he would look as competent as I felt a hospital consultant should look!

We talked. I left a lot of it to Mark, not trusting myself to keep calm. John Wesson was very sympathetic. He wanted to know in detail what we needed and how long for, and what Keston College, the source of my information, thought about it. He couldn't decide then and there. He had to talk to the churchwardens, and by implication, check up on my credentials with Keston, to make sure I wasn't just a loony.

I preached about Irina in several churches around this time. Two women were very moved, and offered to help. Kathleen Higgs was a hospital administrator and Jen Pollard, a retired teacher. On returning from a speaking engagement late on Sunday 2 February, Sue told me that John Wesson had rung and wanted to speak to me. There was no word yes or no. 'Could I ring in the morning?' What would it be this time? If all else failed, I'd go out on the streets and walk until a church would accept me or else walk till I dropped. Whatever happened, the Irina Vigil would go ahead.

Up early the next morning, I waited around on tenterhooks until Sue had taken Christopher off to school and until John Wesson would be in his office. I rang. The answer was 'Yes!' Sue confessed to knowing since the previous night but didn't want to tell me. I then discovered that she had been praying before Christmas that I would not be able to do it. In the New Year she changed her tack and began to feel that if God didn't want it to happen, he could stop me doing it and if he did want me to do it, there was no point in her trying to block it. Sue certainly didn't egg me on, especially considering that she was by now some fourteen weeks pregnant!

If we were to make it for the beginning of Lent, as we intended to, we only had nine days.

I rang round the committee members, including Kathleen Higgs at the hospital in Solihull, calling them to a meeting that night. Nic Mendes put me in touch with Mr Wormington, the Managing Director of an excellent exhibition agency who did a superb job, producing a huge photo of Irina, a summary of her story and guidelines for visitors to the cell who wanted to get involved in the campaign. Mark Goulding, our printer, produced thousands of hand-outs in time to be given out at the start of the Vigil. It was clear that we needed an office. I asked if it was okay to do it from our back bedroom. It wasn't! I couldn't afford to have a hold-up at this stage. Someone suggested St Luke's Church not far from the city centre. I rang John Philpott, the vicar, who said yes straightaway. I could use their spare vestry for the whole of Lent, and install a phone.

Jen Pollard organized a rota to run the office 9 to 5 every Monday to Friday. Kathleen Higgs took over the job of organizing the office, immediately producing a press release, as if she were Montgomery at Alamein.

Mark checked up on the effects of hypothermia and hunger and Mr Harrison mobilized the Jews. Mr Qazi and his daughter Jabina stayed up all night typing, copying and mailing letters to all the Muslim leaders and diplomatic celebrities they could think of. The next eight days were a whirlwind of activity. I had hardly a moment to relax. I began to long for the cage as a place to sit down and be quiet.

Next morning, Sue wasn't feeling too bright so I took Christopher to school, where I met Richard Hendey, a carpenter and father of a girl in Christopher's class. I told him of my project and he agreed to come and fix up the cell once I'd got the materials together. The first scaffolding firm I tried loaned me as much scaffolding as I wanted to make the frame for the cell. They brought it to the church, erected it and took it down afterwards. I bought the plywood for the back and sides of the cell from a timber yard in the city after they should have been shut, and at a knock-down price.

A lighting manufacturer heard me tell my story and dug around in his old stock till he found half a dozen lamps on an angle bracket, which were just what we needed to illuminate the cell and the display boards.

'Weld mesh', the metal mesh used as security grilles in front of shops, was used to represent the bars of the cage.

Mr Beany, the owner of an industrial-clothing shop, gave me overalls for my prison clothes and big galoshes as boots and back in Halesowen, a mountaineering shop contributed a long thermal vest!

British Telecom installed a phone in double quick time on hearing of Irina and a friend covered all the installation costs. George put together a magnificent rota of stewards to oversee the exhibition in front of the cage, to welcome people, answer questions and make sure no one wandered off with the kitty. The stewards also had to check up on me to make sure I didn't become quietly unhinged, particularly at night. I really appreciated them.

Kathleen and Jen and company got all the press releases off to people we had listed from *Willings* press directory, which we'd tracked down in the central library.

A rota of women from the church came and kept Sue company throughout the whole period of Lent. A wonderful service. It was a bit of a strain at first, having a new person each night, but after that these women became old friends.

I told a photographer of our project and he kindly took a photograph of me as I was before having my hair shaved off. It was a 'before' shot to go with an 'after' shot, in case I wanted to show anyone what I looked like before being shorn.

Igor and Irina never had the opportunity to get a 'before and after' series done! But they did what they could. They knew what was coming to them. Thankfully, a friend took them one day and stood them against a stone wall and shot them—with a camera. The pictures are some of the best available of Irina (though not the one on the cover of this book). Igor stands, bearded, a head taller than Irina, his anorak slightly unzipped with a level, steady gaze at the camera. He's a level, steady chap. He needs to be. Irina on his left, her eyes level with his shoulder, and a still slightly impish sparkle in her eyes. They are eyes, however, which convey the significance of the

the photograph of the future prisoner. Wearing a dark coat, she has the hood folded back with the check lining showing. She had an unusual head of curly dark hair, brown or black one cannot tell, it's a black and white photo. A dark spot at first appears to be a blemish on the print but it's in all the photos of this session and turns out to be a distinguishing mark on her face below the corner of her mouth.

The office was run from the Monday before Lent to answer queries from the press. Dad came up and sat in the freezing cold vestry at St Luke's. He took calls from correspondents at *The Guardian*, *The Times*, the local papers and TV and radio who all rang in.

Pancake Tuesday came and went, and Sue and I settled down to our last night together. I came to bed very late, working on our home-made part of the display and last minute bits for the cage. It was a short night. I was up early and off to the BBC for a live piece on the Ed Doolan show. This Australian 'personality' had a reputation for saying what he thought and a few damning words from him could have made it hard to come over well.

I was very relieved when he said, 'There's no way I'd want to knock what you're doing, Dick. I think it's great! I have just one criticism. Who's looking after your parish while you're away? Don't those people need you too?' Fortunately, I was able to explain that I'm not the vicar of the church, just a part-time assistant with leave from David, my vicar, to go and do this.

I had eggs for breakfast and then packed up loads of equipment for the cage and exhibition. A letter-box for letters for Irina; bedding for the night-time stewards and a camp bed. So many bits and pieces. Sue and I piled into the car, leaving Christopher with Pat and Roy next door. He had measles at the time and the sight of his sad little bespeckled face watching me from the gap in the lace curtains of Pat and Roy's bay window was difficult to leave. Was I doing him a great injury? Should I settle down to a more conventional kind of fatherhood? I calculated that in two days after the start of the Vigil, Irina would have finished her six months in solitary confinement. I didn't know at the time that the six months was really five months and that she had returned from the solitary cell some weeks before. She was in fact back in the barracks, although prisoners weren't that much better off in the barracks. Irina was ill and if I knew her by now, it wouldn't be long before she'd be back in the cooler after some other moral triumph.

We were ready to go! However, already something really strange—wonderfully strange—had happened.

Irina's conditions during those five months in solitary were not always the same. It was on 13 November that she finished a spell of thirteen days on the particularly harsh punishment isolation regime, with fewer clothes, no bedding and no exercise. It was bleak, but on 13 November she was able to resume the usual 'camp prison' regime, which meant she could wear rather warmer clothes. Irina was suddenly flooded with a reassuring feeling of warmth. She didn't put it down to the warmer clothes, but to a supernatural feeling that all would be well, a feeling—in fact a knowledge—that people in the West knew about her and that something was beginning to happen.

The day when I mentioned Irina at church, when Anne and I felt so compelled by her story, was 18 November. However, the news bulletin was published by Keston College on 14 November and the news was received a day or two before that date. Irina's conviction that 'people knew' had coincided exactly, or almost exactly, with news of her plight arriving at Keston.

5

THE VIGIL BEGINS

Sue came with me to St Martin's on Ash Wednesday morning, 12 February. We got out of the car, a plump man and a slim woman. On Easter Day we got in again, a slimmer man and a plumper woman.

By that time, Sue was twenty-four weeks' pregnant. I'd lost one-and-a-half stone body weight and a lot of clothes. My anxiety about getting cold made me put on jeans, long johns and mountaineering tights, all under my boiler suit. I soon discovered that it was very cold sitting down. The four layers of clothes cut off the blood supply to my legs, but it was several weeks before I dared shed a few layers and I felt much warmer as a result. Some friends had already helped make final preparations, including people from St David's, our own church. The ubiquitous Michael was fixing things around the cage and Mr Qazi and Ibrahim and Abid, his friends from the mosque, were there as well.

That morning a bearded, dapper man in a sheepskin coat was looking at the displays about Irina at the back of the church. I greeted him. He had a kindly air about him and obviously knew what he wanted. His name was Michael Hart, who introduced me to the team he'd brought from Central TV. I tried to hide my excitement at getting at least one interested party from the media. They were going to do a series of pieces on the Vigil for a religious magazine programme called *Contact*.

With half an hour to go before the time scheduled for the start of the Lenten fast and the shaving off of my hair, I was still fiddling around trying to get everything ready: the displays, the visitors' book, the petitions, newly arrived literature from the printers, and so on. Each time I looked up, there were more people. Paul Hoyland of *The Guardian* came, John Manning of *The Times* and Bill Ellmann, the *Daily Telegraph* photographer. The release of Anatoli Shcharansky the day before had made the whole thing topical in a way I'd never dreamt of.

The porch door opened and a man walked in carrying what looked like a shaggy version of a dachshund on a stick. I recognized who he must be when he was followed by another man carrying a video camera with BBC TV written on the casing. They were an ENG (Electronic News Gathering) crew, who said that a rabbi was outside asking for me. I went out to meet him and his wife, Mrs Singer. He was still convalescing after an operation, but had come to wish me well and to give me his blessing. I knelt in front of him, outside on the forecourt, as he laid his hands on my prison-type cap. The symbolism of a Jewish Rabbi blessing a Christian minister was very important, and captured superbly by the press. Rabbi Singer took my arm as I walked over to a chair outside the door of the church and sat down. Anne, the woman who had wept for Irina three months before, got out an electric razor and started shaving my head. She worked on a neurological investigation ward at the Queen Elizabeth Hospital, and was used to shaving patients' heads before operations. I felt the warmth of the machine buzzing, but not just around my neck as it usually does at the barber's. This time it went up over my head. Michael Hart appeared on the scene, pushing his way through the cluster of press people, and asked the obvious question.

'How do you feel at this precise moment, Dick?'

I might have guessed! I could tell them all about Irina till I was blue in the face but I hadn't rehearsed any reply to this question. I could have said something trite but checked myself. I thought it might not be productive in the long run. I could have said that I was enjoying the publicity, which I was. I remembered the PR people saying, 'Make sure the limelight falls on Irina'. I confessed that I felt embarrassed about my hair, but that I also felt closely identified with Irina, describing her plight.

The razor jammed with my dense, thick locks. Anne cleared out the blades and buzzed on, the Rabbi holding my left hand.

Anne asked, in true barber fashion, is that enough off the top? I put up my hand and felt a fuzz like velvet but punctuated by tufts of hair that Anne had missed. It wouldn't have satisfied a brain surgeon. She trimmed the bigger tufts but I think she was being kind and didn't do a really radical 'Kojak'.

There was quite an audience standing around outside the west door of the church. The cameras and equipment as well as the supporters and onlookers all traipsed inside to see me get into the cage. I had to do it several times to satisfy the cameras.

Then came the photos in the cell. Of course there are no photographs of Irina with her head shorn or in prison clothes and none of her cell or of Podust.

They wanted me to look serious and to hold my glass of water and plate with a piece of dry bread on it. One wanted the two items together. Another had my hands apart in what seemed a most unnatural position, plate held out in one hand, glass of water in another. One chap had a fish-eye lens and took a most startling photo of the lattice work of the grille framing me in my boiler suit on the edge of the sleeping board with my head turned to one side. Again, it felt unnatural but was very eye-catching when I saw it in the local free paper the next day.

There was plenty of coverage—but not much talking, I thought. I was left with the impression that some were after a picture and didn't really focus on Irina. But some did get the right perspective, like Paul Hoyland of *The Guardian*, the local papers and the local radio and national TV. *The Times* and the *Daily Telegraph* did not seem to use the story at all although the prison clothes, the bread and water, the shaven head and the bars all seemed to have made visual impact.

Michael Hart told me, 'It will be hard for you not being out of the public eye for six weeks.' I didn't tell him I would be glad if that came true. Some of the PR people had forecast that it wouldn't attract sustained coverage. I was left with a couple of people whose shoulders sagged under the weight of heavy portable reel-to-reel tape recorders.

They had come for interviews for local radio. Supporters gave their greetings and returned home. An agitated woman started to shout abuse at me and Ron the 'beadle' (or caretaker) came up and had a gentle chat with her. She calmed down and staggered off to get another bottle.

People came and went all afternoon. I spoke to many of them and could squeeze two fingers through the mesh to shake them by the hand; two fingers into their palm! This became a familiar greeting. I nibbled some bread which a Jewish woman had left as the start of my ration. It was pungent rye bread with caraway seeds, and brown, not in the way that we usually think of brown bread. This was a reddish brown and came from a Polish delicatessen.

Lots of elderly people walked by, mostly with shopping bags. Ron told me they were going to the Wednesday Club. Time passed talking to visitors at the bars. The side door of the church opened and the Club filed back out. Some paused to find out what it was all about.

'Oh, a woman in Russia, is it? Yes, it sounds horrible, doesn't it? I wouldn't like to be there. Do you think you'll be all right? Pretty woman, isn't she?'

Kathleen, Jan and George came and we had a short Vigil committee meeting. We resolved to open a bank account. When they went, I was left alone in the church. It was getting dark, and Ron had shut up shop. The last of the praying figures in the pews picked up his plastic bags and shuffled out into the February twilight, muttering as he went, Ron coaxing him on and sympathizing with all his problems. Ron checked that I was okay, told me there'd be an evening service and disappeared into the vestry at the far end of the darkened church.

The contrast with the bustle and glamour of the press conference hit me. I looked round my cell, sorted out my bedding and thought of all the letters I had to answer. I wondered whether the TV was covering the day's events on the early evening news. I reflected on all that had happened and prayed that it would do some good. Was it all an 'ego trip', playing to the footlights? No, I felt sure it wasn't. Irina was in her cell and needed help. We had to make sure not only that her plight got publicity, but that it was of the right kind and enough of it to help secure her release. A little blip here and there would not be enough. The Vigil would have to produce results judged by people writing in for information, writing to their MPs and praying. For months I had longed for a place to put the cell, and here it was—the dream had come true!

Ron came back and opened the doors for an Ash Wednesday evening communion. I could hardly hear a thing in the service. There was some faint singing in a chapel at the opposite corner of the church and I heard the curate talking. Then the congregation filed past the cage to the church hall for a meeting, some asking, some looking and some not looking as they passed. The church was empty again. The lights were out, apart from those which we'd rigged up around the cage. The street lights and the flood-lights kept it from being completely dark. I found this very peaceful, in spite of the traffic rumbling past. The occasional horn sounded, and from time to time groups of youths passed on their way to or from some revelry.

It wasn't eerie. I saw no ghosts and heard no bumps. It felt like home. It was a feeling, I reflected, that the boy Samuel must have felt when he slept in the temple with the ark of God, although of course, he did hear a voice!

A doorbell rang. It was the side door which led outside from the passage to the church hall. Ron was not within earshot so I let myself out of the cage over a scaffolding beam and through a gap I'd left in the side wall. I peeped through the peep-hole and saw a man carrying a grip and a sleeping bag. Undoing the bolt and chain I welcomed Derek Bishop, my 'steward' for the first night.

'We saw you on the tele,' he said. 'Just a little bit, but it was enough and on both channels, I think.' They showed the Rabbi, me having my hair shaved off and getting into the cell, and a picture of Irina.

We fixed up a camp-bed on the parquet flooring in front of the mesh. I took my half-hour exercise period, walking round the church with my companion. The rule was to do thirty minutes of this sort every day, usually running up the side aisle, walking across the front of the church, and back down the other side aisle, a zig-zag through the baptistry at the base of the tower and back to the cell past the main door. I often did it in my bare feet. There was no need of shoes but you had to be nimble to avoid slithering into the base of the pulpit!

Derek and I had a chat and prayed. Then Derek went off to sleep while I got on with answering all my post. I'd been so busy finding the place for the cell that I had a terrific backlog of letters to catch up on. I wrote late into the night. I thought of Irina. She received hardly any post. Very occasionally she got a letter from Igor but in return, the only word to get back to her husband bearing news from the camp was on the occasional postcard. Although she wrote much more than that, the mail was very heavily censored and she could write very little about her progress. Likewise, although thousands of people wrote to Irina from the West, not a single letter got through, or perhaps just one, because she wrote a poem about her unknown correspondent, but that was all! However, the universal plea of released prisoners is for us to keep on writing. 'It shows you care! It makes things better for us!' Michael Bourdeaux, the director of Keston College, has a dictum: 'Your letter may not get to the prisoner but it does get somewhere! You can be sure that it won't be thrown away without the contents being noted, such is the bureaucratic process.'

It was cold in Irina's cell too, in fact much colder when she started her time in the camp prison (PKT). Fortunately, when Irina realized she was to be in this perishing cold cell for many months, she went on hunger-strike until it was eventually agreed to give her some basic heating.

The camp prison where Irina spent her five months' sentence was at Yavas, about ten or fifteen miles south of the 'small zone' at Barashevo. Her cell had four bunks in it, two on either side, hinged up against the wall like bunks in a railway couchette. I get the impression that she spent a lot of time alone, despite the potential for accommodating other prisoners. The idea seems to have been to break up the groups of women who kept supporting each other.

In Irina's cell were an iron table and two benches. The floorboards were rotten and the winter wind blew along the slab of cement beneath the boards and in through the big cracks. A slop bucket was chained in the corner of the cell. The window was barred and didn't fit well. In fact the wind would whistle in through the gaps and often even the panes of glass were missing. If you stood near the window on a windy day, the wind could be seen to blow your clothes around. The roof leaked frequently and the walls were made of cement which was thought to be specially mixed with salt with the object of keeping them damp to the discomfort of the prisoner. Bedding consists of a thin mattress and a single thin blanket which is made of cotton.

The cell door has two layers. Apart from the solid door, there is an inner grille on the prisoners' side, so that the solid part of the door can be opened without the prisoner being able to get out. The prisoner in the camp prison is allowed out usually for half an hour's exercise a day, although one gets the impression that this was not always adhered to. Criminal prisoners in this kind of regime were obliged to work during their time in camp prison. The authorities did not want the politicals mixing with the criminals at work, so they were kept in their cells.

The authorities produce a newspaper as an instrument to try to re-educate the prisoners. The one in Irina's camp was called the *Udarnye Tempy*, which comes out as something like 'Hard hitting tempo'. It's designed to give lip service to the idea that the labour camps are for the reform of dilatory workers into the shock troops of the revolution's labour force. However, as one might imagine, they don't circulate the newspaper in the women's policital zone. They fear that the women would just laugh at it. The camp prison, however, is common to criminals and politicals, and the prisoners all have to sign to say whether they want to receive it or not. They are also allowed to listen to Soviet radio, to read five approved books and to smoke.

Reports differ as to whether the food in PKT is better than on *shizo*, the punishment isolation regime. The slip of paper from the camp which Keston published in 1985 says that the food is the same as on *shizo*—bread and water, with soup included on alternate days.

Back in my cell, I fixed up the thin mattress which I'd

68

got from an old beach bed. It was about an inch thick but it helped. I had one blanket and a pillow, although I didn't know whether or not Irina would have one. Before I went to sleep I had to climb up the scaffolding and lean over the top of the mesh to turn out the lights. I lay there looking up at the vaulted roof of the aisle. The city lights cast a soft glow across the arches. I tried tucking the blanket round me with the edges tucked in under the mattress and I drifted off. A couple of hours later, I shifted my bottom to relieve the numb patch and then lay on my side. I rolled over. It was jolly cold. My feet were inside Mr Beany's galoshes but they seemed to have parted company with my body. I tried to get comfortable but the cold crept in through my back despite the blanket.

A brilliant idea came to me. What was I lying on? The best insulation around. I picked up the mattress and wriggled underneath it, arranging the blanket as best I could, around the whole lot, and I lay face down on the door which formed my bed. I drifted off, to wake up half an hour later with some four hours more to kill and incipient bedsores on the bony bits of my hips. I whiled away the rest of a freezing night, longing for the dawn and recalling the time I shivered for a night in a copse on Dartmoor, under a single blanket. Army Cadet camp with the Marines at seventeen is one thing, but a six-week stint at more than twice that age is a different story altogether!

Prisoners in the women's camp had to wear short-sleeved dresses of striped cotton. Irina was given this material when she first arrived at the camp and was told to run herself up a dress to wear. She got into trouble because she made one that was too long and voluminous and capable of hiding all sorts of things in—anyway it was worth a try!

In the 'small zone' they wear a headscarf of cotton, thick stockings and heavy black boots. Slippers could be worn in the dormitory outside working hours. If the weather was very cold, they were usually allowed to wear a lightly padded jacket, but only down to the waist, and it had no collar.

The punishment cells were very cold as the winter wind blew in through gaps in the floor boards and around the ill-fitting windows, which often had panes missing. The snow would blow in and lie on the inside window sill without melting.

It's difficult to get a completely accurate picture of these cells, but the reality does seem grim. There was only a board to sleep on and even that would be padlocked against the wall by day. One blanket, really only a cotton sheet, would be allowed by night and removed by day. The food was limited to an almost indigestible, thick, gluey, black bread and three cups of water a day, with one serving of lukewarm soup on alternate, 'warm' days.

The food back in the barrack accommodation was better, but not much. No prisoner was given any fresh fruit or vegetables during the whole of her confinement, for years at a time, and no milk, unless on an invalid's diet. Scurvy was rife. Many lost teeth. Natalya developed a rash which sounds like pellagra and many developed oedema or swollen ankles, owing to protein deficiency as in Belsen, as well as becoming very emaciated.

Morning did arrive, eventually. Not even the cold could stop the earth turning. Denis, the senior beadle, arrived soon after seven to find me trying to eke out whatever warmth I could. Derek had had an excellent night. The dear chap snored all the way through! It was nice to have his company. Without it, I think I'd have gone round the bend or jacked it all in even though I constantly reminded myself that Irina had no such choice if she were to remain loyal to her calling.

Denis was worried about the electrics. Looking with a more discriminating eye, I saw that he had good reason to be. Richard came back and fixed it, making us less likely to electrocute anyone as we poked our fingers through the grille.

The cell's framework was an eight-foot cube of scaffolding with oblique bars to stop it all flopping around. The floor of the cell was made of scaffolding boards, heavy timbers which rested on the lowest scaffolding bars and raised the cage off the floor a little. The back and sides were made of plywood, nailed to further scaffolding boards whilst the grille formed the front. The sleeping board was a hardboard door fixed to the back wall on hinges, its front edge propped up by vertical wooden posts screwed to the front corners. A window high up in the back wall looked out on to a view of Irina's own camp—in fact, it was one of the photographs supplied by Amnesty International and pasted to the back wall inside a little window frame.

On either side of the cage looking from the front, two more doors made a handy display surface which we painted black to show off the exhibits. The lights focused on the display boards and cell from projecting bars above the heads of the visitors. To get out I had to slot myself through the gap between the front of the plywood side panel and the grille and then under the lowest display panel. It was quite a tricky manoeuvre at first. The cell was set askew across the south-west corner of the church, so that behind it, in the corner, there was storing space for odds and ends, including a camp-bed for the night-time 'stewards'. I had brought most of the contents of my filing cabinet and all the letters I had to reply to, as well as saws and screwdrivers, and pots and pans for the porridge. I even thought at one stage of installing an office with a typewriter and photocopier!

Mr Harrison pointed out how this must all look through Christopher's four-year-old eyes. He felt it would be great for him to have as he grew up, the memory of his Dad getting into a cage. I'd been worried about leaving him and Sue, and rightly so, but I was glad that someone else could see at least some possible benefit for Christopher arising out of this venture.

It was good to have the opportunity to talk to Mr Harrison. Much of the time in labour camp Irina could talk to her fellow prisoners—the time in the barrack block in the 'small zone' at Yavas. The assortment of women in the 'zone' were from many different backgrounds. They were from many different parts of the Soviet Union: Lithuania, Latvia, and Estonia, the three Baltic Republics were all represented, as were Moscow, and the Ukraine. Differing Christian denominations were represented in the barracks, Catholic, Pentecostal, and Baptist, as well as Orthodox, but they took great pains that no misunderstandings should be allowed to arise to enable the authorities to set them against each other. They realized very early the potential problems that could arise if they let differences among them develop. There were some interesting professions represented. One woman was an architect, there were two teachers, a church organist, a seamstress, a theatre director and, perhaps most poignantly of all, a former lecturer in Marxism at the prestigious bastion of communism, Moscow State University. Galina Barats had now become a Pentecostal Christian. The barrack block where they lived together was an L-shaped single-storey building. The longer arm was the dormitory with two rows of bunks. It used to have a wood-burning stove, but this was replaced in 1978 by a system of radiators.

They ate in a dining-room which, strangely enough, was equipped also with a television which received the ordinary Soviet TV programmes. In the base of the L was a sewing-room where the women had to make industrial gloves all day. The noise was terrific and they were not allowed to go for a break.

Sue and Christopher arrived at lunch time. Sue was very composed. It felt very odd giving her a kiss and talking to her through the bars. Sue had bought Christopher a new box of 'Lego' which he played with on the floor in front of the cage, ignoring me at first. After a few minutes, he asked if he could creep through under the display into the hidden space just outside the cell. He perched on an oblique scaffolding bar, chatting about all sorts of things and asking questions as he looked round the cell. I showed him how I slept and where I went to the toilet and washed, and all sorts of things that a four-year-old needs to know. He wanted to see it all, so I took part of my half-hour exercise period for the three of us to go exploring. I discovered that I could open the front of my boiler suit a bit and hold the opening over the nozzle of a hot-air hand dryer in the toilet. It was bliss. The hot air inflated the suit and blew me up like a Michelin man or an astronaut! The warm air blew down my arms and legs thawing them out, and creeping across my back. I felt a bit guilty doing this, especially as I thought about Irina, but argued that surely real prisoners find ways and means of easing the situation.

I had slipped one of the people at the cell a bit of cash

to buy a bunch of flowers for me to give to Sue. She appreciated this very much and as a family we felt close, despite the strangeness of meeting like this. Christopher was still measley but recovering and it was his half-term from school.

During the day I developed a headache, the sort I usually get on holiday after I start to relax. My body considered this a holiday! I couldn't face eating the pungent rye bread. I became nauseated and faint and hung my head back to look at the ceiling, which often gives some relief. It felt as though an express train were thundering through my head, and I was about to vomit when I heard distant voices beyond the grille speaking to each other.

'He must have tremendous stamina,' one woman said to her friend. I didn't disagree with them, although I felt as weak as a kitten and wondered how on earth I was going to get through another forty-five days of this. I rallied a bit towards evening and worked out what I considered to be another crafty dodge. I found a bit of stiff steel wire left over from fixing up the lights. The way I was using the blanket, I could only benefit from a single thickness. So I doubled it over and sewed the folded edge along one side of the mattress by poking the wire through each in turn. It was a pretty coarse job, but it helped me to sleep far better, even if only for three hours. But this was enough to shake off the worst of the headache, so that by morning the world seemed a much brighter place.

That Friday was, I felt, the first productive day in the cell. Previously, it had all been a bit of a whirlwind, and at times a dead loss. Now I could take stock. It was a busy day, with lots of people to talk to, who came by and reported what they'd seen on TV or read in the paper. *The Guardian* included a picture of my head being shaved and a bit of blurb, though not as much as Paul Hoyland had sent in. The local papers all covered it as did both TV channels in their local news magazines. Almost everyone wished me well. Only a few came to argue and I decided not to rally to such challenges. Usually the other visitors took care of them for me.

The Vigil provoked people to make all sorts of comments, such as:

'What about the old people who haven't enough money to keep warm in the winter?'

'What about South Africa?'

'What about the unemployed?'

A couple of Irish chaps came by one day, swearing and pretty tanked up. They told me all about Bobby Sands. I just sat it out and eventually, once they had had their say, they went on their way.

These were all very much the exception. Most visitors were very positive. Some were quite shaken. At one stage a senior clergyman came and wept at the cage over a family tragedy. Several women kept coming back to tell me about relationship difficulties or some family grief and to ask me to pray for them or their relatives. Friends, neighbours and relatives came. And others just came in out of the cold. It certainly was cold that February; the snow lay on the ground for several weeks with the muddy grass in front of the church frozen hard. I allowed myself to go outside for my exercise period but in practice hardly ever did as it was so bitter outside. I wondered how Irina survived in conditions more extreme than mine.

Outside her barrack block in the 'small zone' was a pear-shaped compound encircled by fences, the dormitory end of the block facing towards the apex of the pear. The whole ensemble was barely sixty metres long and was flat with a single watch-tower at one corner. There were only twenty women inside at the most, except in the early seventies when the 'zone' was overcrowded. More recently, it has taken only seven or so prisoners, Irina being one.

There is a shelter in the compound—a roof on four poles, with two long troughs for washing clothes. Near the troughs is a water tank. A path runs round the edge of the area, and beyond this is a garden plot and then three encircling fences, two of barbed wire and one high wooden one with barbed wire on top. Over these you can identify the camp psychiatric hospital which is a single building. A hospital for prisoners with TB lies by the gate giving access to the 'small zone'. The whole 'zone' lies tucked into the corner of a much larger camp for women criminals.

The whole camp complex was developed shortly after

the 1917 Revolution, but I imagine that the individual buildings are more recent.

The food in the dining-room of Irina's barrack block was pretty basic. The prisoners had three meals a day but the diet is monotonous and vitamin deficient. There is a dish like rather poor quality porridge for breakfast and lunch, or sometimes they get noodles with a little butter. The evening meal is made from fish or pork, but the fish is not gutted or scaled and the pork has usually gone off. It's pretty putrid. Usually no one eats it until they get so hungry that they are prepared to risk being ill in order to get something into the stomach. The food is very salty. Apparently, the salt ration is 25 grams a day. Often it is added to the prisoners' diet whether they want it or not. This amounts to four or five lightly heaped teaspoons, which must be revolting to taste.

The garden plots are intriguing. There is a statutory weight of vegetables which theoretically the diet must include. The garden plots were originally allowed for growing flowers; vegetables were not allowed. However, an understanding arose that since the kitchens could not or would not supply the required amount of vegetables, the prisoners should be allowed to grow some in the flower beds during the summer. But that all came to an end in August 1983 when Podust, the section leader, ripped up the plants with her bare hands.

A Polish visitor to my cell stressed that camp-life is tough. Irina's camp was no exception. In the sewing-room they had to produce seventy pairs of industrial gloves a day.

The sight of the cage certainly had a sobering effect on many people. Some friends came and said, 'Oh, Dick, I don't like seeing you in there.' One dear friend wept and for ages couldn't come near me. Most of the time I wore a woolly cap which hid my shorn head and kept me warm. With the cap off, my fuzzy head felt strange, just as a new-filled tooth feels out of place. I ruffled the stubble on my scalp, brushing it against the cold steel bars of the weld mesh.

Most days I was busy from the moment the doors opened at 9.30 a.m. to closing time at 4.30 p.m. There was always someone to talk to. I had a faithful band of stewards by day and night, organized by George. They were recruited from far and wide. My own church was very loyal, as was my family, who came and did a great deal.

For some reason, a conversation sticks in my mind which I had with my father about the war. I asked him how he managed to make a home for himself in the most uncompromising surroundings of North Africa, where he was an army surgeon with the Guards. In a particularly muddy winter, he managed to make a good bedside mat out of the wing of a Messerschmidt that had crashed near their field ambulance.

It was often difficult to give time to relatives when so many other people had come, often from some distance.

Most awkward of all, though, was not being able to give Sue the attention she deserved. Often she would come in with Christopher and combine it with a bit of shopping and then have only a little time to spare on the parking meter. It didn't go down well when one day the news people were there and I felt torn between attending to them and attending to Sue. I longed to see her and Christopher and yet the news coverage was important too. To tell the reporters to go away and come back in half an hour seemed to be tempting providence a bit. After that Sue and Christopher would come at closing time, when we would stroll round the church, arm in arm, or I would race Christopher up the aisle, across the church and back the other side, or go and see the 'hot-air blower' in the toilets! He often lingered and had to be prised away at the end of a visit, sitting on the scaffolding on the edge of the cell. I wouldn't let him into the cell itself. I felt it would be breaking unwritten rules, as Irina would certainly not have all this family contact.

Sue bought a couple of little toy chicks with furry heads popping up from an eggshell. They squeaked as you shook them up and down. She gave one to me and one to Christopher. I sat mine on the scaffolding at the side of the grille inside the cage and Christopher brought his with him when he came to visit me. His chicken could talk to my chicken so they wouldn't be lonely. It was a stroke of genius on Sue's part and it worked.

He didn't have any severe upset at school or at home. Sue found it more difficult coming to see me, because of all the work involved in a family expedition with Christopher three or four times a week when she was pregnant, the fag of finding a spare parking meter and usually getting Christopher home to bed late.

Things became routine at the cell too. My appetite returned and I developed a real liking for the Polish rye bread. Visitors always volunteered to go over to the delicatessen to get me a loaf when I needed one. I only once had to ask. They were 900-gram loaves. Irina was said to have 450 grams a day, so I made sure my loaves lasted two days. They were kept in a plastic bag to stop them drying out too much, and I divided them by digging my fingers in and breaking off a hunk. The half loaf broke into three fistfuls, one for breakfast, one for lunch and one for tea. Sometimes I was late eating lunch because of the queue of visitors, or letters I was trying to get in the post. Sometimes I kept back a bit for a late-night snack. I got a few hunger pangs at first but they settled on water, a good slug of which proved remarkably sustaining. I kept to the dietary regime of 450 grams of rye bread (or other bread) per day and a bowl of porridge on alternate days. The porridge mornings were also the fresh-bread mornings. Sometimes the bread was warm from the oven. Those were the good warm days, which Irina would never have known. The porridge, a bowlful without milk or sugar, tasted insipid, but filled me up for an hour or two. A couple of pounds of oats lasted for six weeks.

After a while I became quite a discerning bread connoisseur. The loaves were sausage-shaped, stumpy 'baguettes'. Pull off a pinch between your fingers for each bite, munch well and take your time about it. There's great variety within one loaf, the crust at the edge and the pulp in the middle, which is delicious in those Polish loaves. Occasionally you hit a seed and savour the aroma as you crush it in your teeth. The bottom of the loaf has a tougher and more chewy consistency, to exercise your jaw muscles and tax your back teeth. Then there's the mushy bit at the sides, often a little under-cooked and juicy. Why settle for roast beef and two veg when you can have half-a-dozen different experiences from a loaf of Polish bread washed down with beautiful Welsh water from our Birmingham taps? You have to eat it slowly though, or it will stick in your throat.

A Polish woman came by who had been in a labour camp in Siberia under Stalin. She despised my venture.

'The real bread,' she said, 'has bits of string in it, bits of bones, and mud and stones. It's not cooked properly, and you have to work hard to get a little of it.'

She poured out abuse which I tried to take graciously. Another passer-by came up and defended me without being asked. The Polish woman spent her anger and after a long time changed her tune, announcing to all around, 'I respect this young man for what he's doing.' She was quite right in her comparisons and I would make no claim that my conditions were anything approaching Irina's, particularly the hot-air blower, the illicit stitching of the blanket and the snow-boot liners at night.

The nights got much better, although I never slept more than about three hours, thereafter waking and sleeping fitfully usually lying face down with my hands on my hips to stop getting sore over the boney promontories. As I lay awake, my feet were always perishing cold. The galoshes weren't the answer. Somehow they got sweaty without getting warm. I decided the rules were a bit vague about footwear in the camp prison, as far as I knew them. Though I must admit, I didn't do any fresh research to decide whether this was legitimate or not. The liners from a pair of snow boots were a great help. Funnily enough, I found that if my toes were warm, I could stand being a bit cold over the rest of me. I just wriggled harder to keep warm.

On the first Saturday afternoon, Helen Lloyd came to me with a tape recorder slung over her shoulder. She recorded a bit for the *Sunday* programme on Radio 4.

She asked all the right questions—about Irina, about the cell, what I wanted people to do. She warned me that they always edit it savagely, and off she went to Pebble Mill studios to pipe it down the line to London.

A wedding came and went, without seeming incongruous. Anthony, my brother-in-law, arrived for the night and we settled down to sleep eventually after I'd written loads more letters. It was a rather bleak evening. I was fortunate to have access to writing materials, and someone who came especially to keep me company at night. Again I was painfully aware that Irina would not have had these luxuries.

The cold was a problem. Before I dared to wear a bit less, my clothes were so tight when I sat down that my thighs felt cold where they squashed against the edge of the chair. Also, the boiler suit was too small and pressed down on my shoulders and up into the crutch. This was not deliberate but perhaps it was fairly authentic. Someone told me that a form of torture sometimes used is to dress the victim in tight clothes and then wet them so that they shrink. I can see that it must be very unpleasant.

All this created a dilemma. I wanted to stand up to keep warm because my clothes were more relaxed that way. It was comfortable all day because I stood up almost all the time, talking at the grille. It seemed rude to sit when my visitors stood. However, I could not write the letters I needed to write if I stood up. The only solution was to write so furiously that I wouldn't think of the cold.

In the evening I arranged beds for myself and the steward. After a chat and a prayer, I would go off to sleep. Even this was a luxury. Irina wouldn't necessarily have anyone to pray with—certainly not on a regular basis.

The local commercial radio station, BRMB, rang in the morning and I did a brief phone piece with Chris Allen, who had once been the curate at St Martin's. He helped a lot and rang me for a live 'phone piece' for his programme each remaining Sunday morning of Lent. Anthony brought in a little radio—another concession. We tuned on to Radio 4 and discovered that we were on the *Sunday* programme, practically unedited. They even gave our address at the Vigil office at St Luke's Vicarage. This generated a hundred letters a day after that for most of the week, spreading the news about the Vigil all over the country. It was the single most important piece of publicity we had throughout the campaign.

What seemed to register to people was my claim that

God had told me to do this. Sunday services came and went. It was good to see the people, and church was pretty full for the main service. I couldn't hear the smaller services in the side chapel. They seemed desolate and remote from the opposite corner of the dark church from where I was listening.

Monday morning saw the start of what was to become a routine. My visitors included Mr Woolworth, the multi-millionaire, who was a delightful man. He'd come up and sit by the grille and show me his drawings, which he pulled out of a plastic carrier bag. They were crayon drawings of stylized religious themes. Mr Woolworth was always good-natured, except one night when Ron tried easing him towards the door at closing time. He trundled out muttering to himself and didn't bear a grudge when he came in at 9.30 the next morning. He had a heavy overcoat, an educated accent and a cheerful bobble cap with a tie wrapped round it. He would frequently pray for Irina in marvellous eloquent prayers which were absolutely to the point. God heard your prayers, Mr Woolworth. Later, when Irina arrived and I had the opportunity to invite people to Lambeth Palace, I would have loved to have brought along my good friend Mr Woolworth, bobble cap, tie, and all. To my shame, I didn't have the nerve.

My friends and I realized that we needed to keep the impetus up. The media wouldn't come back just for an update. Lying in bed on that first Monday morning, the idea came to me to issue a call to the churches throughout the country to observe three dates for Irina: 4 March, her birthday; 16 March, Passion Sunday; and 27 March, Good Friday. I issued a press release to the effect that with 53,000 churches in Britain, I hoped that twenty per cent would respond on the first date by sending me a card to say they'd prayed for Irina, fifty per cent on the second and ninety per cent on the third. The *Church Times* and the *Methodist Recorder* both included my request. I called a press conference for that Friday and hurriedly sent off notices to bishops and other church leaders to outline the idea. After the *Sunday* programme, I had high hopes and waited for the Friday press conference with anticipation. Then came the real low point. Friday 21 February, the day of the great press conference. No one came. Not a soul. I'd not been able to get to a phone to chase up the press and someone who was going to do so for me ultimately didn't find the time. We'd sent two batches of press releases, which to be fair, several papers used without coming in person, but it was really depressing.

We rang to find out why no one had turned up. They told us, 'While he's in his cell he's covered. When he comes out we'll do a bit.' One programme said, 'No, we're not interested in covering it. Of course, when you get her here that's a different matter, we'd like to know and we'd probably do a bit.' Angry, I resolved to go into *shizo* (the punishment cell) and to reproduce the conditions—vest and shorts, no mattress, only a blanket which was removed by day. Actually, I now discover that often there is not even any blanket in the Soviet cells.

Mark Taylor, my doctor, wasn't too bothered about this but Mr Harrison felt it was a bit much. There were other avenues we hadn't tried yet. I prepared a press release to say I'd go into *shizo* regime the following week, but delayed sending it. It would be terribly cold. Was Mr Harrison right?

It was a miserable time. I thought I was getting nowhere. I was irritated and everything was getting on top of me. Finally, I gave in to pressure from many friends, and agreed not to go ahead.

I remembered that 'human anger does not work the righteousness of God.' Mr Harrison rightly said, 'You've got nothing left after that; all the media people can say then is, "If you could kindly burn yourself to death, we might give it a mention on the news but we are not promising anything."'

Disgruntled but relieved, I ditched the idea, slung the news releases in the bin and turned in for the night, though I did keep a few copies just in case.

6

THE WORLD STARTS TO NOTICE

That was the low point.

But Harry, my American neighbour, arrived and read a bit out of the Bible and we prayed. I hadn't been reading the Bible as I imagined that Irina wouldn't have one.

I sat up in bed and for once I was really warm. My confidence had been at a low ebb. All of a sudden that changed. I developed renewed confidence that I was on the right track, that what I'd said on the *Sunday* programme about God telling me to do all this was true. I began to understand what the Bible says about anger not working the righteousness of God. My angry outburst could have wrecked it all. After it was all over Irina commented that personally she found that it was vital never to be consumed with hatred or anger towards her captors. Whatever the apparent stubbornness of her dealings with the authorities, she claims they were never motivated by hatred or rage. She didn't need to lose control like that. She had a poise and confidence which arose from a knowledge that she was doing what was right.

What I re-established was the confidence that I was on to something with a power and persuasiveness all of its own. I was so glad that the Bishop had said no to the Cathedral churchyard plan, because two weeks into it would have brought me to this same low point. Fortunately, I still had a month to go, now that I was doing it for the whole of Lent. I didn't have to end on a 'down'. All this helped me see the little gains and to be glad of them.

Some had already occurred, and in my anger I'd not really taken them in.

On the previous Friday the Assistant Bishop, Colin Buchanan, had come to visit me at the cage. He used to be my theological college vice-principal and had only recently been made a bishop. He encouraged me a lot.

The same day I had another unusual visitor: a Chinese man, who spoke quietly about his family, his job and his country—not in the way we English people do. There was a dignity about him that was unmistakable. He was not sullied with the banality of Western life. As we talked, he looked round, pressed his face up against the grille, lowered his voice and said,

'I came to tell you that three months ago I became a Christian.'

This was the most important thing he'd ever discovered in his life. It was his jewel. He'd found life—what it was all about. He begged me to keep my voice down and not to tell anyone.

'It would be dangerous for me and my family in China,' he said.

I opened my mouth to reply but no words came out. I turned to the wall and hid my tears. How I loved and respected this gently spoken man for his courage! How I grieved that although China is now portrayed as being much more open to Western influences, this man knew what it's like under the surface! I could smell the fires of persecution on him, almost as a physical sensation. He obviously thought that the man in the cage would understand, even if no one else did. It was a profoundly humbling experience.

Another Chinese Christian was to seek me out much later, on the eve of his return to China. We went for a drive so that we could talk. I pulled up at the kerb in a quiet street. For several minutes, he dithered about whether or not to go back to China and cast himself on the mercy of the local Communist Party officials. He knew he would be sent for 're-education' and I could see him shiver with fear. I heard his voice—the voice of a grown man falter and tremble as if he was going to cry. I assured him that he could stay with us if he so wished and we would look after him. I saw some tears, but in a minute or two he regained his composure, wiped away his tears and resolved to return to his land at their mercy. He asked to be left at a bus stop, and that was the last I saw of him.

How could I afford the luxury of depression and stagnation when people like this were facing such trials?

I continued to have streams of visitors. A man who had been in prison told me that in real solitary it is terrible —the walls press in on you. In the camp prison, Irina had streams of visitors, too. The only trouble was they were not the kind of visitors she wanted! It was very important, she says, to see who was coming to see her. If it was the doctor, she had to take off the towel which she wasn't supposed to have tucked round under her dress to keep her warm. If it was the assistant commandant, she had to hide everything on her body because he always searched around the cell. If it was the commandant, she had to hide her books because she had more than the permitted number of five. They used to search through the ones they could see to see whether she'd written any poems in them.

I depended a lot on my visitors, especially Sue and Christopher of course. How Irina must have longed for times like these.

Another ring at the door and I recognized, illuminated in the glare of the bulk-head lights, the distorted form of the editor of a local newspaper, viewed through the fish-eye lens of the security peep-hole. He'd been meaning to come for some time apparently. We had a good chat and he wanted to help. He thought they could do a feature if I could think of something from Irina's writing which would answer the question, 'Why should the average Midlander bother about her? Is there a message from her writings for us with our problems?'

I could see that he had to sell his newspaper, but the conversation brought home to me the parochial interests of the media in Britain. I couldn't think of any message Irina could give to unemployed Midlanders except perhaps the courage to make the best of their circumstances. But he did give me a useful tip: 'Prepare a dossier about Irina, and send it round to the press.' We did this. It may have helped, I don't know.

That morning I prayed that we would make some progress towards getting into the national press within a week.

And at eleven o'clock, some four hours after that prayer, the BBC World Service rang and arranged to put out four broadcasts about Irina in *Report on Religion*, which would go all over the world! I heard later that a friend who had just emigrated to Israel heard it loud and clear. Perhaps more importantly, the Russians don't jam the World Service as they do the BBC Russian Service. It's said the senior Communist Party officials and the Politburo like to listen to it so they know what's going on in the rest of the world!

There were other advances as well. Just after I started in the cage I wrote letters to all sorts of people in the performing arts, as well as MPs and church leaders who I thought would be interested, asking them if they would be 'patrons' of the Vigil. The replies started to come in. Brian Forbes and Nanette Newman (husband and wife) were the first to reply. Sir John Mills and Janet Suzman backed us up, as did Isla St Clair, Frank Muir, Maggie Smith and Sarah Miles. Later on, Hayley Mills wrote back to apologize that she'd been away and was she still in time?

I was so grateful to all of them. Elaine Page, Diana Rigg, Judi Dench, and Bamber Gascoigne replied. David Kossoff, the reader of the imaginative Bible stories, encouraged me a lot.

Susannah York would have liked to have come up to Birmingham to show her support, but she couldn't make it because of prior commitments. So she got in touch with friends who were performing in a Birmingham theatre at the time. I was minding my own business one morning when a press photographer suddenly appeared from nowhere. A quick exchange informed me that Susannah York's friends were on their way round from a rehearsal of the play *Ross*. The door opened and in walked a troupe of actors. They were very considerate when I could not immediately name them all. (I'd dreaded someone really famous coming to see me and not being able to recognize him!) There was Simon Ward, who was in the city playing the leading role in this play about Lawrence of Arabia; David Langton of *Upstairs, Downstairs* and Ernest Clark of *Doctor in the House*. They were really good value and posed for lots of photos.

Richard Briers wrote back to say he'd be a patron and could he and his wife come up to see me from London? They came just before Easter and were most thoughtful. He had just taken part in reading a 'roll call' of Jews who were being prevented from leaving the Soviet Union. That event was given tremendous coverage in the media. The Jews are very experienced at these things and do them very professionally. Christians have a lot to learn from them. The local television covered Richard Briers' visit well. He said he had come because he wanted to stand up and be counted as caring for prisoners in Russia. Frankie Howerd rang and gave some tremendous support.

All this boosted my morale greatly. At least the press, even if they hadn't plastered their pages with coverage of this event, had not ridiculed it as I feared they might. And now that I had some famous sponsors I could list their names on the phone when I rang the press. At least when they said 'no', I'd feel less paranoid about it, knowing that I had some distinguished supporters!

I say 'ring the press', but at that time I had no phone. I began to feel terribly cut off in the cell, and imagined again how Irina would be feeling. We organized a birthday cake and a little celebration for her birthday on 4 March, although hardly anyone from the press was interested.

I got fidgety. I delegated the ringing to various different people. Some were too nervous and timid. Some were too pushy and some forgot.

My feeling of isolation grew by the hour. I couldn't even get letters off easily and we were receiving loads of them. Fortunately, most were dealt with by the willing helpers at St Luke's. But there were some which needed me to reply. At first, I tried to write them by hand and got tired. Then I had great ideas of a secretary who would come in each day and bring back the typed letters in the evening. The nearest we got to that was an arrangement whereby I dictated on to a machine and George ferried tapes back and forth, bringing back the letters typed by various helpful people in the suburbs. They did a good job but the letters took nearly a week because they were all busy people. Eventually the answer was to get out my biro and get on with it by the old steam method. It had the advantage of keeping me busy at night so I didn't think of the cold and went to bed exhausted with writer's cramp to think about instead of frost-bite!

My sister Mary and I put our heads together about the telephoning problem. Rightly or wrongly, I wanted to be able to speak to people in the media first hand. How? A 'cell-phone', though appropriately named, would have been prohibitively expensive. Very promptly, and at our request, a telephone surveyor came out to have a look and recommended an extension from the phone in the vestry. The church kindly put up with the inconvenience of having the vestry phone disconnected. An engineer came the same day and laid festoons of cable along the side of the pews underneath by the central heating pipes and over the arches of the church doors and we were in contact!

I rang Sue to celebrate and asked her to check by ringing back. Promptly, three callers intervened, so she could make no reply and was a bit confused about her elusive husband! She felt it was a bit of a liberty my ringing her at home when I was supposed to be in prison. I figured that I would not be talking to people all day through the grille if I was really in prison so a phone was only another step in that same direction. But it did raise a few eyebrows when visitors saw a phone in the cell.

The support built up from other quarters, too. Several religious leaders expressed their support: the Bishop of Coventry, the President of the Methodist Conference and the leader of the Methodists of the Shetland Islands, who became a patron. I was particularly delighted about that. The leader of the Baptist Union of Scotland did the same.

I sent a circular to all the Anglican and Roman Catholic bishops and the equivalent Methodist and Baptist leaders. The Catholics responded with one patron to join the Church of England's Bishop of Coventry. The Baptists provided two General Superintendents. The Methodists came out top by producing four patrons from among their District Chairmen!

On the other hand, Mr Arieh Handler, Chairman of the National Council for Soviet Jewry, came to visit me in my cage as early as the eighth day of my fast. He had just returned from Israel where he had welcomed Anatoli Shcharansky on his arrival from a Russian prison camp. A senior member of the Board of Deputies of British Jews, June Jacobs, also came to see me. She brought a book about Jews in Russia and joined Mr Handler on the Board of Patrons of the Vigil.

Mr Qazi came up trumps and brought his Muslim priest along with an entourage. I was really touched by this gesture of support. He gave me a blessing as I knelt before him. I came in for a bit of criticism for associating with the Muslims, but if they were good enough to help Irina, I was glad to receive them.

Even the Dudley Branch of the Communist Party supported Irina. They were moved by the news of her situation and all decided to send her cards in prison to encourage her. They brought me along a placard which read, 'Dudley Communists Support Irina' and put it on the grille. They were a delightful bunch of young people.

There was no falling off in the number of visitors. Most came to pay tribute to Irina or check up on how I was. Many wandered in from the market outside, even though our professional hoarding had long since disappeared. A lovely black nurse came from the children's ward of the hospital where I'd been working, along with one of the ward sisters. Elderly ladies came in to see me who had not made the trek into town for years! Nuns sent a message to say they were praying round the clock for Irina and me. A television producer wrote to me pretending I was in prison, referring to my guards and the date I'd get parole and so on. He included a sticker of a dove identical to one he'd sent to Irina.

Kids sometimes teased me with sweets or chips, and I suppose the same scenario came Irina's way when she was on hunger-strike. There was a time in August and September 1983 when they went on hunger-strike and the guards showed them white bread, eggs, butter, sugar and other goodies. As soon as they stopped the hunger-strike, however, all the goodies disappeared!

In fact, you could get some sweets in the camp shop. It opened twice a month and you could spend your meagre earnings there if you had any to spend. They sold poor quality caramels, margarine, white bread (better than the rough, heavy black bread on the usual menu). Also on sale were toiletries, combs, pens, paper, exercise books and stamps.

Anyone not working to the norm would lose privileges. Almost certainly, they'd lose the opportunity to buy goods at the camp shop and anyway they wouldn't have any earnings to spend there even if they were allowed to go. They could also easily lose their right to correspondence or to receive their one and only parcel. Prisoners in the first half of their sentence were allowed to receive one parcel a year weighing up to a kilogram. That's not much, and it wasn't allowed to contain anything of much value to the prisoner, especially no meat, chocolate, vitamins or medicines. After serving half their sentence, they are allowed a five-kilogram parcel annually—not much of a concession.

They can also easily lose their rights to receive a visit from a relative. Strict-regime prisoners such as the women in the 'small zone' are allowed three visits a year, though this is more often denied than granted. They are also supposed to be able to write two letters a month, but then again they often go astray or offend the censors. They can't say anything much about themselves. In the camp prison, the correspondence is cut down to a letter every two months but again in practice a lot of these don't get through.

I began to have dreams. I dreamed of a pork chop one night towards the end of the Vigil, and frequently craved for a joint of beef and a log fire to sit by!

I also had a nightmare about a press conference I'd arranged and to which no one came. Another night, I had a vivid dream about the layout of the cell and then I flew to the sun through coal smoke rising from the chimneys of alms houses, in an aeroplane bristling with electronic aerials. Then it turned into a balloon and I was living in great luxury on a thick-pile carpet on the floor of the gondola of the balloon, with suburban Britain spread out below. Then, all of a sudden, we were in the back streets of some place that was not quite Birmingham!

Sometimes they fished me out of the cell. One

morning, one of the clergy forgot it was his turn for taking the communion service, so they asked me to come and take it. I made a start and preached a sermon. Then he arrived, so I got back in the cell. Another night my medical expertise came in handy. The youth club was having a party in the church hall when a lad cut his arm quite nastily, so they asked for my help.

Another time, I was asked to speak at a lunch club about Irina. So I got together some of her poems and my own story, waited till Sunday lunch was over, then came and talked. They were kind enough to clear the food away before I arrived and to have Sue, Christopher, my sister and her whole family to lunch on the house.

Central TV came back to do the 'half-way through' bit. Nick meanwhile interviewed me with Michael Hart directing it all in the background. It was the first time I'd seen what they do if they only have one camera and want to get pictures of the interviewer asking questions as well as the interviewee responding. They run straight through first and a secretary takes down the questions in shorthand. Then they can go wherever they like. Nick stood in the nave with the back-drop of the altar, asking the same questions into the air with no reply from me in between. Then it was put together in the studios.

They came back in the afternoon when Bishop Colin Buchanan returned to do a piece for their programme about the service of 'footwashing', re-enacting what Jesus did on the first Maundy Thursday. He came in a simple cassock with a flash of purple to show that the person washing the smelly feet was none other than an Anglican bishop. And whose smelly feet did he wash in front of Michael Hart's camera? He washed eight feet, belonging to a black couple, an elderly white woman and me. He had explained that I was someone taking part in a 'vigil'. I wanted it to be a bit more precise, but Michael Hart said quietly and finally, 'No'. So I somewhat ashamedly held my peace and let the Bishop wash my feet, with due apologies that I'd not washed them since the day before!

John Wesson, the rector, came in for a morning service on Sunday morning, 9 March.

'Did you see it?' he asked, smiling. A big article about Irina and the Vigil in *The Observer*. Half a page, with a picture of Irina on the front page.

I got given several copies of this newspaper by passers-by that day. It was a masterly piece by Blake Morrison and opened the way for more.

'Today,' it started, 'in Birmingham, a thirty-eight-year-old Anglican clergyman and orthopaedic surgeon will complete his twenty-sixth day inside a cage, and on prison rations . . . Dick Rodgers' vigil ends at Easter; Irina will not be free again until 1995.'

I had to watch that I didn't get too proud of myself. For a start, I think it was Irina's poetry supporters who put Mr Morrison up to it, so I couldn't claim any credit. But it was great! The message was getting round, and the excellently researched article painted a vivid picture of Irina's plight.

All this time there had been no news of Irina herself —not since the original article in November. Even that was old news in that it reported a six-month sentence starting in August, which was due to be completed in February, and in fact finished in January. However, with my new phone, I decided to find out a bit more. By ringing Chicago in the middle of the night, I was able to catch Yefim Kotlyar as he got home from his job as an engineer in that city. He and Irina had been friends in happier days as students in Odessa. Yefim had never met Igor, but did a good job of keeping in touch with him by ringing his Kiev apartment from time to time. We had a good chat which was rather expensive, but I couldn't have done it from the coin box in the vestry!

Irina's blood pressure was high, so Igor had heard in a letter. She had swellings, he didn't know where. The temperature of her cell was around ten degrees centigrade *above* zero not ten degrees below, as had been published in this country. I think this was a misunderstanding of the Russian. It came as a bit of an anti-climax to hear that the temperature of her cell was at this level. At first I felt, 'What's all the fuss about, plus ten degrees centigrade isn't very cold!' Then I realized that this was about the lowest it

91

ever got to at St Martin's, and most of the time by day it was around seventeen degrees centigrade. It made her conditions much more realistic, ten degrees below had never really been credible. I mean, sitting in a deep freeze in your underwear would surely spell death. While ten degrees above is more possible, it must really get to you after a while, idling away the days in the depressing, chilly cell, with the cold gnawing at your thighs and a hole in your stomach. I now knew that from my own experience.

Time was precious. I had less than three weeks left and we needed more coverage if the thing was to do Irina any good and reach a level of interest that would continue afterwards. I decided after all to go into *shizo*, the punishment-cell regime. I felt happy about it this time, wanting to try conditions more closely resembling the punishment cell.

This regime is pretty tough. They call it *shizo* (an abbreviation of 'punishment-isolation cell' in Russian). The cell is the same kind as for PKT, the camp prison, but they take away the prisoners' dresses, headscarves, stockings and shoes. The dress provided is very thin and short and has lots of holes through which the guards can see whether the prisoner has managed to put on any non-regulation clothing that she's smuggled in. It's very cold without a headscarf and with no heating. There is a radiator but it hardly ever works. The winter draughts blow in from the window and the cracks in the floor. The roof leaks and the walls are damp. The bunks are padlocked away during the day and there's no mattress or even any blanket. The temperature is not supposed to fall below sixteen degrees centigrade without the extra provision of quilted jackets . . . but it does. It goes down to as low as eight degrees centigrade which must be very cold with a bare, shaven head and short-sleeved dress riddled with holes. The temperature is measured every day by the guards and it is always sixteen degrees centigrade—according to the guard's coil thermometer anyway. One day it was put down on the inside window sill in the unmelted snow which was lying there and it still registered sixteen degrees centigrade!

Once Irina and Tatyana conducted a survey of the cell

temperature, after smuggling an alcohol thermometer into the shizo cell. Whenever the guards used the coil thermometer, the reading was always the same—sixteen degrees centigrade. They also used an alcohol thermometer but preheated it. Then they would put it on a cloth to insulate it and they'd read it so quickly that it had not fallen to a true reading. The day-time temperatures were usually around twelve or thirteen degrees at a time of day when the guards sometimes recorded temperatures of over twenty degrees. Once they recorded twenty-six degrees when Irina made it twelve degrees. The guards took no readings at night or in the evening but the temperatures at night were usually about eleven degrees, which is very cold when you have so few clothes. Indeed, once in punishment conditions she did not even have a board to sleep on and had to lie on the cold concrete floor.

In *shizo* there were no books, no comb, sometimes nothing to wash with. The diet was very bleak. On the cold, empty days when there was no soup it must have been very depressing. Other prisoners elsewhere have reported receiving food only every third day. Irina says she heard the criminals in the next cell complain that the soup was always cold.

'Look,' they pointed out, 'the fat on the top of the soup has always frozen by the time it gets to us.'

'That's simple,' the commandant retorted.

'From now on, we'll make sure there is no fat in the soup.' (Of course it's the fat that gives what little benefit the soup provides.)

The worst thing is the enforced boredom—having nothing to do, nothing to read. Irina managed to work. They never succeeded in crushing her creative spirit. They knew she was a poet, yet she still managed to write in prison, and in *shizo*, where she had nothing else to do, she wrote even more. She had little paper but she devised a great method of artistic expression—soap. She got hold of anything with a small fine point with which to scratch her writings on the surface of the bar of soap. They never found out. She kept the poem on the soap until she was sure she'd got it in her brain. Then, when she'd rehearsed it many times and not made any mistakes, she washed her hands and it was gone.

My plan was to spend a week boxed up, unable to communicate with people. It was quite different from the last time I'd considered it. The first time I was angry and my anger drove me to it. My friends were wise to dissuade me. This time it was out of solidarity with Irina and they did not even try to talk me out of it. I'd have the same kind of clothing restrictions as prisoners in *shizo* and the same bedding. Richard, the carpenter, put up a roof and a front wall of plywood, to enclose the cell completely. We made a hatch in the front to get in through and a window of one-way mirror glass. This seemed a bit weird, but it was the only way in which I could be cut off, but still allow visitors to have something to see. I decided not to talk to people in order to preserve some sense of isolation.

It was going to be cold. I wore what I thought would be roughly equivalent to *shizo* uniform—vest, shorts and socks. In fact, I was soft on myself because mine were knee-length socks and a thermal vest, but I dispensed with my hat and my thighs were bare.

The food stayed the same according to the message on the scrap of paper which Keston had received from inside the camp, so I continued on bread and water and a bowl of porridge alternate days. The bedding arrangements were a bit grim. I lost the mattress. The sleeping board and a single blanket were available at night only. (It turns out it should have been only a cotton sheet rather than a blanket.) The board was folded against the wall by day. Mark, Douglas and John, my medical friends, checked up on me during this week. They insisted that I take my temperature every two hours and write up the result on a blackboard (it was actually my bedboard painted black), together with the room temperature in the cell. At first, I had to do this all night. Sue made me promise I wouldn't go ahead with it unless all the gaps in the stewarding rota were filled before I started. She and others were quite worried that I'd go hypothermic. The business of writing up my temperature on a board was partly to make sure I was still doing things and thinking straight, so that they could fish me out if I wasn't. I agreed in advance to stop if Douglas told me to. It was a great additional burden on the stewards but the gaps were filled.

So on Friday, 14 March I slipped round the back of the cell into the junk area and changed into my running shorts, while Richard finished off boxing in the cell. I got in through the hatch after a bit of encouragement from friends and some prayers. For the first few minutes, I just sat there looking around, surveying the scene. The two-way mirror was embarrassing, not so much because of having people looking at me but because of what they might think. It seemed to be another step towards insanity. I could see movement if I looked at the window. If I had come right up to it, I could have seen out through the narrow unsilvered gaps between the strips of mirror which faced my way and reflected my image back into the brightly lit cell.

A bulb had to be burning all the time inside the cell so I could be seen both by onlookers and by the stewards who were keeping an eye on me. I was aware of people craning their necks to look in through the two-foot-by-one-foot 'window' to try and see where I was.

'I can't see him, can you?'

'Yes, he's down there sitting against the wall.'

'No, he's down at the other end; I saw him a few minutes ago.'

I felt like a lesser-ringed Indian marmoset, or some such animal, in a cage at the zoo, spending most of its time hiding in a corner.

Some would come and ask, 'Are you all right, Dick?' They called out again and again, but I couldn't answer—or wouldn't. It was agonizing, especially when people didn't understand or forgot. Some got really upset and confused by it. I heard from several women afterwards that it really disturbed them to see me cooped up like that. Nevertheless, it was the nearest thing most of us are likely to see to a real Russian Christian in a punishment cell.

After I had sat for a bit and explored the cell, I made a little pocket on the wall for the thermometers out of sticky tape taken from the floor and arranged my can of water. I then worked out all the geometrical patterns of the tape on

95

the floor and had my bread for lunch. After that, there wasn't much to do.

I sat on my bottom with my legs out straight on the floor and thought. My thighs got cold and goose-pimply. I brought my knees up against my chest. My feet slid away, my socks sliding on the smooth paper with which I'd covered the rough floor boards. I folded my arms round my shins and buried my chin between my knees and went off to sleep, trussed up like a chicken. I awoke half an hour later (I had an alarm-clock to tell me when to take my temperature). It was two o'clock, so I put the thermometer under my tongue—thirty-seven degrees centigrade. The afternoon was scaring. I couldn't think what to do with the time. I was intrigued with the idea of a whole week lying in front of me with nothing planned, no letters to write, no phone calls, no family to visit, no books to read, nothing.

Mind you, I could hear people talking—talking about me, talking to the steward, explaining what it was all about. The phone rang and it all had to be explained again. I heard Sue and Christopher come and someone scrambling around kicking the plywood. I could guess which one that was! I didn't hear Ron's footsteps but he came and locked the church door and it all went very quiet, and rather terrifying. A few more minutes and someone drew back a chair, paced around for a bit, looked at the temperature reading I'd just written up, and said something to acknowledge it before entering it as a dot on a temperature chart.

Nine o'clock and there was a lot of scratching, scuffling and rattling on the grille. The hatch opened to reveal Douglas with a portable chemical toilet, a blanket and a jug of water. I put up the board and screwed the legs on with a screwdriver I had kept in the cell. With nothing better to do, I wrapped the blanket round me and lay on the board after saying my prayers. I could only get one thickness out of the blanket like this. The burning of the 150-watt bulb in the confined space kept the temperature up to about seventeen degrees centigrade all night so it never got really cold. We needed the bulb to do the readings (although admittedly not such a powerful one). It was a chore in the middle of the night to respond to the alarm clock and do a reading,

96

wriggle down to the end of the board and write it on to the edge facing the window so it could be seen. I slept perhaps half an hour at the most at any one stretch that night and time dragged. I didn't need the alarm. I never slept that long.

We had agreed that if the body temperature dropped below thirty-five degrees, I'd accept a sleeping bag to warm up in. It dropped to just thirty-five point two degrees on several nights. It made me anxious and agitated but never confused. I've never been able to sleep when cold. Without a mattress, I couldn't get comfortable that night, try as I might.

In the morning Douglas advised me to do regular exercises to keep warm. I touched my toes fifty times and did twenty-five knee bends and ten press-ups every half hour. It did keep me warmer. I walked round the cell one way then the other, my head brushing past the bulb. It wasn't a long walk. The cell was about seven feet wide by four from front to back. The bread I divided into smaller portions so I could break up the day with elevenses, after-noon tea and a late night snack each of which consisted of a piece of bread about the size of a matchbox—but they tasted good and if I ate slowly they relieved the boredom.

I discovered the best position to sleep in, on my tummy with the blanket doubled and the edges folded under my hips and shoulders. The sleeping board itself offered enough insulation to stop my front from getting too cold. It left my feet cold, but I'd got used to that by then and after a while, we cut down on the night temperature readings once I was obviously going to be okay. Sunday dragged and the evening emptiness was forbidding, but on Monday morning Harry Hewat, my American friend, decided that I'd like him to read me a bit from the Bible. He couldn't check with me that this was the case, but just went ahead and read Psalm 136. When he had finished that, he paused, carried on and read Psalm 137, then all the way through to the end at Psalm 150. After that, he read me the whole of the Sermon on the Mount—Matthew chapters five, six and seven. I could hear it all perfectly well inside the cell. It had a tremendous effect on me. It was very encouraging indeed to find that someone outside was not intimidated by the box I was sitting in—but just kept communicating with me, even when I could not acknowledge what he was doing.

On Monday my arms ached and I dropped the press-ups. The rest of the exercises became much easier as I was getting fitter, but my thighs ached with the unwonted exercise. My elation helped me think more usefully. I began to treasure the time in the cell. I didn't know when I'd have the opportunity to spend a week with my own thoughts again. I thought I'd better make the most of it! So I started to think of cameras. I'm crazy about cameras and buying lenses, and special film and learning to develop and print my own films. I spent the morning, between exercises and temperature checks, day-dreaming about all this, about learning French, going to France, and about happy childhood camping holidays in sunny southern Europe. Then I thought about Sue and how lucky I was to have her and how lovely she was, and Christopher, and what a delight it was to have a child and another on the way, and how I'd have to be a better father and a more loving and helpful husband. How lovely it would be to go on holiday with Sue when I got out of the cage!

Tuesday was a porridge day and my knees started to click and creak with all the exercises. The afternoon was dreary and when the church closed, it was oppressive. I started to count the days. I'd chalked them up on the walls of the cell all the way up to forty-six and crossed them off as time went by. In the open cage, the time had flown and I'd almost had to restrain it, with all the visitors by day and the interminable rush to get letters and press releases in the post by deadlines. Now in the closed cell, the days loomed large and slow. I wanted to push them by and they wouldn't budge. In the empty evening, squatting awkwardly in the corner hugging my thighs, self-pity gripped me by the throat. It was overpowering. I tried to pray. Usually if I feel down nowadays, I can get solace in this way, but it didn't come then. I realized how awful it must be for Irina and others who don't even have families—those who always face long, oppressive evenings alone. I squatted on the floor, huddled face down in a bundle to keep warm and to concentrate. I felt the outrage that although I was in such a cell in the comparative warmth for a week, Irina had served at least 138 days in far colder cells amid threats and with no prospect of any more human treatment in the foreseeable future.

Then, outside the cell, Dot Berry began to sing. She wasn't very tuneful but it was obvious she was singing not for herself but for God and for me. She must have sung a dozen songs and hymns. She then went through a card index of Christian prisoners, praying for them all by name, aloud. I could see it was a card index because I was curious and found myself having a little peep through the clear stripes in the mirror. She was illuminated in an otherwise darkened church, so she showed up. Dot and Harry were parables to me of the need for people in the West to go on trying to get through to people in prison, to encourage them even when, for years, they can't respond—I can tell you, it was a very powerful parable to me.

After that the time did go by, slowly but inexorably. I reduced the exercise to cope with my aching left knee. By Thursday, the boney bits in my bottom became rather sore because of sitting on it so much of the time. I tried all sorts of positions and spent more time pacing around.

On Friday I heard lots of movement outside. An American friend, Margaret, had taken on the job of telling the press when I'd be coming out and evidently she'd done a good job. I opened the hatch, wriggled out between the grille and the front wall, and then took a bit of 'exercise period' while friends took the front wall away.

It was a wobbly feeling standing and walking amongst the reception committee. I felt exposed and vulnerable, like a chicken coming out of its egg too soon, but it was a jubilant occasion. The local papers were there. A correspondent from the main Norwegian evening paper, *Aftenposten*, had come to do a major story for their last issue before Easter. He was a tall, slim, softly spoken man who boasted that Norwegian newspaper technology was a 'little bit more advanced' than that in England. Soviet affairs are very important to these Scandinavians who have a frontier with the Soviet Union.

My European MP Christine Crawley was there and spoke very encouragingly of developments in the Council of Ministers. And of course there was my Dad, bless him! He always turns up at the right time, even from London, at the age of seventy-eight!

They put me on the air on Radio Free Europe, the American service covering the Soviet Union. All this elation seemed like the end of the Vigil—like the end of term. But it wasn't. There were eight days to go, and time dragged. I got near to breaking the dietary rules and nibbled into my next meal's ration of bread—but never into anything I shouldn't have beyond that.

There was a brilliant reading of Irina's poetry on the Sunday by poets who had come from all over the place. David Constantine, who shares a birthday with Irina, had written a most moving poem and Elaine Feinstein read in her slow, measured tones. Teresa Cherzas came up for this from the BBC Russian Service in London. We discussed the whole scene for believers and other dissidents in Russia and I remember her pithy comment:

'You don't have to have as many people in prison as Stalin did,' she commented, 'to control the population, as long as people know that when the chips are down, that's what will happen to them if they step out of line.'

The present release of comparatively large numbers of prisoners needs, I'm sure, to be seen in the light of Teresa's comment.

On Saturday Bishop Hugh, the Bishop of Birmingham, came to see me at the end of an anti-apartheid march. It was great that he had eventually made it to the cell. He let us take a photo of him at the bars of the cage and he sounded enthusiastic. He was perhaps still not completely sold on the idea of this Vigil, but was coming round to it by degrees. My two other sisters from London and Liverpool came to see me with their husbands, which was a great joy. I wanted to write to every MP about Irina to ask them to sign the Early Day Motion. So my sister Sue and her husband Nick got down to it and together we signed, packed, sealed and stamped letters to all 650 MP's—quite a feat for a quiet Saturday afternoon.

After being in *shizo*, it was quite hard to get down to writing letters again. I'd forgotten how to write at first! But by Monday, I did a press release to say that I was about to complete the forty-six days of the Vigil. Paul Hoyland came to have a chat and to prepare a piece for *The Guardian* that weekend, but at the same time I noticed that Sue and Christopher had been waiting while I'd been talking with a distressed woman. Sue only had ten minutes left on the parking meter and wanted to have a few minutes with me before she had to go. I was frightened of losing Paul Hoyland, so I asked if Sue could go and feed the meter to enable Paul and me to have ten minutes together to put an article together for the end of the week.

Arriving at the meter, Sue noticed a traffic warden's hat bobbing along in her direction and decided that her erring husband's advice might not be timely. In a huff, she got in and drove off home with Christopher in the back. But Christopher wanted to see his Dad and Sue felt pretty bad about it all. A mile down the road, she turned back and re-appeared. Paul had finished by then. We made up to each other and had a nice time, but it all erupted again that evening during an hour-long phone call and *The Guardian* didn't use the article after all!

There was no bath or shower at St Martin's. But I did have a good wash regularly. When I had one on Good Friday morning, I was suddenly struck by how thin and gaunt I had become around my bottom and hips, like a starved Indian cow on the Oxfam adverts.

The *Today* programme did a good interview that morning. They felt it was an appropriate day to do it. The three-hour service came and went. I felt it sounded rather easy, talking about Jesus' crucifixion and not feeling the nails yourself. On Easter Eve the church was beautifully decorated with flowers for what they called a 'walkround', at which visitors came to admire the flowers in readiness for Easter Day. There were so many people that I did not go to the loo for ages. I was so embarrassed to leave the cell empty and make Lynne Pulvermacher, the steward, have to explain to the gathering crowd that I hadn't really made a break for it! When I eventually did go, I had to push past a small crowd to get back into the cell!

Roger Hutchings rang from the *Sunday* programme at Radio 4. They wanted an Easter message the following morning. I was glad of the coverage, but I'm never very good at thinking of Easter messages. It sounds too religious, somehow. Easter Eve and Easter night came and went, and the clocks turned forward. As arranged, a friend from our road came to pick me up early and take me round to BRMB, the local commercial radio station, for a jubilant broadcast. I awoke after a sound sleep. Ordinary 'prison conditions' were really cushy after the week in the punishment cell. I'd slept in a bit, and had to hurry to be ready for my lift.

The bell on the side door rang. I slid out of the cage, let Jill in, and within a minute, we were off in her Chevette round the Bull Ring roundabout to the studio in Aston. It felt weird being out and about—cold and a bit wobbly.

A cheery interview with Chris Allen followed, and then Jill took me back to the church and the safety of my cell, just in time for the phone call from the *Sunday* programme. Clive Jacobs, the presenter, came on the line and asked me the questions we had rehearsed the night before. It was rather odd having a conversation which was almost scripted but not quite. I felt I didn't give of my best as I described the crisis in the cage when Dot Berry's singing helped so much. My previous radio conversations had been less formal. However, when I rang Mum and Dad, they said it came over all right.

I realized I'd taken no photos of the cage myself, so I popped out, climbed up the balustrade, got some pictures from unusual angles and then whiled away the time with some rather unpalatable porridge as the last minutes ticked by till 9 a.m. Anthony, my brother-in-law, cleared up the camp beds where he and my nephew Peter had slept and went off to the kitchen in the church hall to make some scrambled egg!

7

THE NATIONAL VIGIL

My watch ticked round to nine o'clock. I photographed my left wrist holding the camera in my right—to mark the instant. Nothing happened! I'd made it! My nephew Peter brought in the plate of scrambled eggs which was very tasty, but it was the roast beef and two veg that I was really looking forward to.

Sue and Christopher arrived, too, and lots of St Martin's people greeted us. We stayed to the first service before setting off for St David's, our own home church. Would you believe it, it was snowing! Christopher and I demolished our first Easter egg before we'd got three miles down the road into Selly Oak! Sue drove, as the ten-stone weakling was not to be trusted at the helm!

The service had already started at St David's. We crept in at the back during the vicar's sermon. He spotted us and asked, 'How's your voice, Dick? Come and say something!'

I scampered up into the pulpit in my very unclerical-looking boiler suit, sporting a six-week-old growth of fuzz on top, and a scraggy apology for a beard under my chin. If you'd seen me under the arches at Charing Cross with a bed of cardboard boxes, you'd have kept your distance!

I can't remember what I said. For once, I was almost lost for words. I hope I thanked people for their help, not least by continuing to pay me for one day's parish work a week even while I was in the cell.

There were lots of greetings afterwards in the hall over coffee—and Easter eggs galore. One lady gave us a catering tin of fruit salad and a couple presented cash to take Sue out for a nice meal.

It was good to be home. A familiar domestic sight of

washing drying in front of the sitting-room fire greeted me. Sue had cooked roast chicken. My serving was tiny, not enough to keep a small bird quiet, a tiny bit of chicken breast and a sausage or two. We said grace, and I sat with my knife and fork poised to savour the moment.

The phone rang. One of the national newspapers wanted a photo of me having my first meal after the fast. I hesitated. It was pretty good of them to turn out on a Sunday. As far as I could tell, it was the only coverage I was going to get—at least with a picture. It wouldn't go down well with Sue—that much I knew! They wanted it down at the church, six miles away, a picture at home wouldn't do. I reasoned that I had to go and do some clearing up anyway. So I set off to St Martin's with some friends who were going to pack up the cage, leaving Sue to get ready to set off for the Cotswolds when I returned.

I took my plate of sausages, carefully balanced on my knee in the car. The photographer took some good pictures of me tucking into the sausages in the church vestry, with the little gothic window in the background, returning an hour or so later with the prints, some of which were wired down to London.

I hadn't really realized that I was weak until I began to join in breaking up the cage. Then it hit me, and I had to content myself with being ordered out of the way and fiddling around with bits and pieces which had to be sorted out for taking home. I worked terribly slowly and eventually said I'd better get off home or Sue would be worried. Douglas dragged me back from going off to catch a bus, pressed a fiver into my hand and ordered a taxi. It was the first time I'd ever arrived home by taxi. I sat back and enjoyed it all the way. By five o'clock Sue had nearly packed up the car. She was remarkably patient, but it was getting late and things were just a bit tense.

There was a knock at the door. The photographer from the local paper wanted a picture of the convict's home-coming. Under a bit of protest, the family sat on the sofa for a mug-shot. Sue found it hard to oblige with a smile. She stared straight at the camera, looking like death. I'd have liked her to lean into me a bit but it wouldn't come.

'Could you give us a nice smile, please, Mrs Rodgers? Come on, that's better . . . '

But it wasn't! I was trying to hug her closer to me when it happened. You would have missed it if you'd blinked. It was a start she'd have been proud of in her days in athletics. She bolted for the door, slammed it behind her, slammed the door from the hall into the kitchen and from the kitchen to the garage. The garage 'up and over' door rumbled down and under.

Eyeball to eyeball with the photographer, I felt rather helpless. It sounded weak and passive when he came out with, 'I'm sorry, what did I do?' So we contented ourselves with an all-male affair; Christopher giving his Dad a welcome home with a hug and a kiss on the cheek. It actually came out beautifully and what's more they printed it! The other one would have satisfied the records department at Holloway Prison but it wasn't quite the 'welcome home' shot that they wanted for the local rag.

I stuck my nose outside the front door to see whether it was safe to come out. The dust was settling. Sue was finishing packing stuff into the car as if she were Mohammed Ali in a prize fight. Verbal communication was obviously going to be a bit risky and my decision for discretion rather than valour was probably wise. Someone brushed past me, out of the front door and down the drive, with a murmured farewell. I could see the relief on his face as he reached the sanctuary of his parked car. They get the news pretty fast at the *Post and Mail*. He seemed very eager to get his film developed and onto the editor's desk! I don't know whether it was a works car but it had pretty gutsy acceleration!

Sue and I started talking to each other again as we drove over the narrow bridge on the Avon at Stratford. Domestic peace was reinstated by the time we reached our destination—a very chic Scandinavian-type log chalet, not far from the Cotswold village of Chipping Norton. We relaxed together on the sofa in front of a roaring log fire. Our hosts sat us down to a rustic meal. I couldn't resist tucking into the mountainous slices of turkey, but they gave me cruel cramps and colic. Sue was good enough not to crow over my misfortune and the turkey tasted fantastic!

After this, I had a bath, the prospect of which was bliss, though as I lowered myself in, I realized I was sitting on bone, having lost so much weight.

I thought of Irina. After only six weeks in the cage, I was free and she was still in prison. It had been a privilege to enter into some of her suffering. I just hoped it would do some good.

We drove into the village the next day. It was easy to feel like a celebrity when I opened the door of the newsagents. I was sure they would have seen my picture in the papers! Well, of course, it wasn't on the front page; the discerning readers like this sort of thing on the inside pages, I thought. I bought several of the papers and leafed through them to see how each one had dealt with the story.

The first one had nothing, but then it was not a quality paper. The next one didn't major on it either. In fact none of the papers said anything about it at all—not even *The Guardian*, with whose correspondent I'd spent the time when Sue had trouble with parking arrangements. The paper which messed up our first meal together didn't even use the photo of me and my sausages! I remembered what one paper had said when we'd rung the press when nobody turned up to that press conference. 'While he's in the cage, he's covered. When he comes out we'll do a bit,' they had said.

We booked into the Queen's Head in Newbury and enjoyed the luxury of all three sitting in bed together in the evening watching the portable colour television.

This holiday helped to heal us and draw us back together as a family. Christopher was intrigued with having his Dad back. His brother-to-be was beginning to stir in Sue's womb. I was getting stronger, and was able to drive when we returned to Birmingham at the end of the week.

The next question then occurred to me. What do you do *after* living in a cage for six weeks? The answer was easy—be normal. Take Christopher to school, rather more now that Sue was finding it harder to get around. I waited at McDonalds for a distressed tramp who'd seen me in the cage and wanted to talk to me afterwards. He didn't come. I spoke at a meeting in southern Derbyshire which made quite an impact. It was the first group I'd spoken to after coming out of the cage.

On the way back, in the dark, I felt uneasy. Was I, from now on, to be the man who'd spent six weeks in a cage? It was fine for a few weeks, but would I, in five years' time, still be the man who had been in the cage? It wasn't enough. And it didn't seem to have done any good yet. Communications were difficult, but as far as one could make out, it hadn't benefited Irina at all. There was no news of any change in her circumstances.

I rang the House of Commons. The support for our Early Day Motion was building up, so that was good. The barrage of letters that we had sent off from the cage had now boosted the list of signatory MPs up to a hundred, eventually topping 130, which is pretty good for a motion like that. In such cases, the Foreign Office takes note of it as a measure of Parliamentary back-bench concern, as does the Soviet Embassy.

Central TV did their follow-up bit about the cage, this time at the studios in Nottingham. I then took myself off to London to meet some of the people who'd shown interest. The *Church Times* and the *Church of England Newspaper* had helped a lot. The Great Britain-USSR Association sounded a good thing to join and the director received me very warmly in his office overlooking the gardens of Buckingham Palace. There were lots of meetings to speak at, all of which I enjoyed, but clearly this was not the way forward. I organized a party to say 'thank you' to all the various helpers. It was a fiasco. I forgot some of the most important helpers and the whole atmosphere was pretty depressing. To add to the gloom, two of our best helpers went down with cancer.

Then the committee met. There was no news of Irina and it was painfully obvious that we'd all run out of steam. However, at the party there was a lady called Jackie Dunton. She came along to the next meeting and inspired us to keep going. We wrote to loads of people around the country, inviting them on the last day of June, to get into cages, or do something else visual to draw people's attention

107

to Irina's continuing plight. Jackie reckoned it was time to let others do their bit too. We dreamt up a plan for making a simpler cage than the one at St Martin's. The picture we worked from showed a sort of clothes horse clad with wire netting around three sides with a plywood sheet for a back. It looked convincing enough, and lots of people copied our design. In the face of some design faults that later came to light, I had to admit that the original idea existed only in my mind. I'd never actually made this new cage. Yet most people seemed fairly happy with it.

While response was building up, we discovered that two delegations were shortly leaving for Moscow. The Archbishop of York was leading a delegation of church leaders. I got a list of the delegates and wrote to them. About half responded, some very favourably. They did plead for Irina by name in the Kremlin, and in front of a senior member of the Council for Religious Affairs, the official state body whose responsibility it is to control church affairs.

Lord Whitelaw led the second delegation which consisted of MPs. They met Mr Gorbachev. On their return, they would not say whose names were on the list which they left with the Soviet leader. Lots of people by this time were writing to their MPs who in turn often passed on the letter to the Foreign Office. The letters back were signed by Tim Renton, the minister responsible. I received large numbers of them sent on to me by other supporters. At the same time, a lot of the Early Day Motion letters sent direct to MPs produced a steady flow of letters from the Foreign Office which the MPs sent on to me.

They all bore a certain similarity. Each would read,

'We take a close interest in the human-rights situation in the Soviet Union and are particularly concerned at the continued maltreatment of many individuals who seek to exercise the fundamental freedom of religious expression and practice.'

It came from a word processor, the occasional paragraph being changed from time to time if something really new cropped up.

It was a disappointment at first, but I realized that this

chap couldn't possibly give all these letters personal attention. There were too many, and a minister has to be careful what he says personally, so a standard letter would safeguard him as well as proving a time-saving device.

The chief press officer of the Church of England encouraged me to bring my cell down to London to get Irina more publicity. Taking his advice, I got on the train and came down to have a look round. St Paul's Cathedral might have been good but it was a bit too far from the West End. I then made for Westminster, pacing round St Margaret's Church, and its immediate neighbour, Westminster Abbey. I felt I had nothing to lose, so I wrote into the various authorities suggesting sites which seemed to me to be eminently suitable for a cage.

There were snags. St Margaret's was the parish church of the House of Commons and the churchwarden is traditionally always Mr Speaker. They were very sympathetic but said it was not feasible as they had had some embarrassing demos there in the past and it had put Mr Speaker in an awkward position. The Abbey said they couldn't oblige because of security arrangements for events over the summer. This didn't seem so plausible to me until Prince Andrew and his bride walked almost directly over the patch I'd chosen—I conceded to myself that their refusal wasn't that unreasonable after all! So I settled on Speakers' Corner in Hyde Park, but the rules obtaining at Westminster City Council didn't encourage a prolonged stay. I felt I had trodden this path before, only this time I was a long way from home and further from a ready-made team of helpers, who in any case, were getting a bit worn out. Jackie's idea was definitely the right one for now—lots of smaller demos for others to do all over the country.

Finally, news came about Irina. Igor and Irina's mother had both been to the camp again. This time it didn't sound at all good. They were turned away again, of course, but this time she was being punished apparently for not standing up when a doctor came to see her! What the camp authorities didn't admit was that her blood pressure was now sky-high, the lower reading being 150 when it should be about 70 or 80. Probably, the reason she didn't stand was that she was then too ill to do so. The authorities didn't want Igor and his mother-in-law to see Irina because they didn't want news to get out about how bad she looked.

I can't really imagine what it must be like to travel a thousand miles at considerable expense, taking time off from work, and then just be stone-walled. I wonder what Igor said to the guards who turned him away! Of course, by now it had happened as many as six times. Six fruitless journeys and six journeys back home and back to work without seeing her face.

Once Igor was at the railway siding near the camp when Tatyana was being led away to the railway wagon in transit to the solitary cells for refusing to wear the regulation clothing.

It's interesting to see that the camp authorities' action seems to assume that news won't reach the public in the West and that there will be no outcry. If they became aware that they had to keep up a good image, with the political high-ups breathing down their necks, then surely this kind of treatment would rarely happen.

It was good to see others take up Irina's case. The Poetry Society in London's Earl's Court put on an excellent evening at which all sorts of people, well-known in the world of the arts, paid tribute to Irina by reading her poetry. It was also the unveiling of a very good new English translation of a collection of Irina's poems by David McDuff, who introduced the evening. The book is called *No, I am not Afraid*.

There had already been a volume of her poems published in America in English, French and Russian. It was probably this book which irritated the KGB so much earlier during Irina's imprisonment. This was the first definite news of publication of her works apart from in unofficial circulation in the Soviet Union. One day a KGB officer came to her, furious as he told her of the publication of her poems in the West.

'The West will do you no good. You'll be sorry! It will only get you into trouble,' he said.

I expect had he not been so irritated, he would not have given her that gratuitous bit of information and therefore encouragement. The gulag flourishes in the dark.

Roger Lloyd Pack read, and so did Edna O'Brien and Blake Morrison, whose *Observer* article did so much to spread the word around. They read to a packed audience of a couple of hundred as they stood in front of the first-floor window of a house in Earls Court. Many signed a petition to the Soviet Embassy, writing to the Archbishop of Canterbury asking him to employ on Irina's behalf the services of his special envoy, Terry Waite.

It was also interesting to watch little indications of how the occupants of the Kremlin were thinking about Irina. On 4 May, while we were over at a vicarage in Smethwick, our hosts had the radio on. Dr Georgi Obatov, a leading spokesman for the Politburo, was answering questions on the BBC Radio 4 phone-in programme, *It's Your Line.* Once the Chernobyl questions had subsided, a woman rang in and asked Dr Obatov why Irina Ratushinskaya was in prison for her poetry—a good question! I remember his answer very clearly. He listened politely and then said he had never heard of her. He offered to find out about her when he got back to Moscow. I gave him a few weeks and then wrote to him, care of the Kremlin. I never received a reply, although someone else did. A few weeks later, a friend of mine went to a meeting organized by the Medical Campaign Against Nuclear Weapons at which a representative from the Soviet Embassy was explaining the Russian position on disarmament. John made the point that the credibility of the Russian position on foreign policy and disarmament was inextricably linked to their performance on human rights. The official gave a reasoned defence of the Russian record compared to that of Western countries. At the end of his response, John said quite quietly, 'I'd be more reassured if I heard what you have just said from Irina Ratushinskaya.' The response was reflex—as if he'd been touched on a very raw nerve indeed! He said that she was a criminal and was reaping the just deserts of her crime.

There was no point in asking a supplementary question, the point had been made. Something was going on inside the Kremlin. These ambassadors of Soviet foreign policy had been briefed about Irina. This was not quite the change we wanted, but it was there for the asking.

Caroline Moorhead of *The Times* wrote a fine piece on Irina in the regular Amnesty International 'Prisoner of Conscience' column.

Leslie Crowther and his wife took time to help, too. He came and read Irina's poems at a crowded church in Bath where we were hosted by a remarkable Belgian priest, Yves Dubois, an Orthodox who had brought a bus load of his people up to the cage in St Martin's. He prayed deep-throated, haunting Eastern prayers and gave me an icon. His people prayed half-a-dozen times every day for Irina. No wonder there had been some thinking going on inside the Kremlin.

More news arrived on 15 May. Irina has developed severe chest pains and she blacks out in her cell frequently. She is short of breath on the slightest exertion and yet is required to work. She has pain behind the eye, thought to be due to haemorrhages in the back of her eye. She has inflammation of the ovaries, long-standing infections of the kidneys and a chronic fever. She was losing consciousness in her cell. Her fellow-prisoners feared that she might soon die, yet the camp commandant had told her that there were no facilities to treat her in the camp and she was not going to be transferred to a proper hospital. Igor would not be allowed to send her the necessary drugs, which he'd have a job to get anyway. There was no time to waste. We had to press on with the campaign as hard as we could. It had to go wider. We had to work at better co-ordination with supporters and groups in other countries. I had written to all sorts of people and groups I'd heard of in America, continental Europe, Australia and New Zealand before I left the cage. I wrote again when I heard of her deterioration, adding a lot more addresses and inviting people to campaign further for her release.

We produced a lot more literature and a postcard pre-addressed to the Soviet Ambassador in London. That went down well. It was easy to fill in, and people started asking for them by the hundred. Several got rid of 500 or 1,000. The Ambassador must have got sick of them. The Jews invited me to speak at their synagogue. A bishop asked me to

112

talk about Irina down in Truro. It was a long journey down that long, thin peninsula, even on a summer's evening, though it really bucked me up that a bishop should pay for me to go that far in order to talk about Irina.

We were staying in a friend's caravan in Wales, when we heard that the vicar had preached about Irina on the Sunday before! He came to see us, pedalling up the hill on his push-bike for a chat and a cup of tea in the van! Word was getting around, even in rural Wales. Irina's story was receiving wide coverage at last, in the Welsh church press and the *Methodist Recorder* on one hand and in *Cosmopolitan* on the other. I wanted to make sure the message was still coming over clearly at the centre, too. It was time to ask the Minister of State, Tim Renton, if I could come and see him at the Foreign Office. He kindly agreed and fixed a date two days hence to fit in with my plans to speak at a church in Kew that same evening.

I thought I'd make a day of it and went down on the train in time for another look around. I decided to look at a place which had been much in my thoughts —the Soviet Embassy. I entered Kensington Palace Gardens at the southern end near High Street Kensington tube station. The police on the gate didn't stop me. I strolled up the leafy avenue, eyeing the grand embassy buildings of the court of St James. As a rule of thumb, the political repression of any state usually seemed to be proportional to the size of aerial on the roof of its embassy. Our near-European neighbours didn't seem to bother with an aerial at all. Perhaps they didn't mind the British listening in as they phoned home. Others had enormous contraptions rigged up, reminiscent of the rigging on *Cutty Sark*.

I heard that the Soviet Embassy had two main parts, apart from the consulate at the end of the street on Bayswater Road. Numbers thirteen and eighteen look at each other on either side of the avenue. It is closed to through traffic, so on a sunny summer's afternoon it is quite quiet. I walked up the east side past the Soviet Embassy, which has a slightly decaying atmosphere about it. The little tower and big shuttered windows stare at you like a blind eye. There's no decadence about the railings and the remote-control catch.

That seemed to work. As officials approached and spoke into the intercom on the gate-post, the gate would buzz and give access. Sometimes no word was required - I couldn't see where the TV camera was stationed. The gate of the building opposite had been left open. I didn't want to attract attention, so I kept going until I reached the north end of the avenue and out on to Bayswater Road. I was disgusted with myself. I ought not to indulge in this amateur cloak-and-dagger stuff. I turned back down the other pavement until I got to the open gate. It was a baking hot day, and it appears Russians feel the heat too. The Embassy front door was open. A young man sat inside at a small, dowdy reception desk with the TV monitors in front of him, showing that I'd just been on television again! I introduced myself by name, saying I was a clergyman concerned about Irina Ratushinskaya and asking to see one of his superiors. He ushered me to sit down opposite him in the lobby on a plastic-upholstered settee on Soviet territory. Out of the open door, I could still see the outside world. Close the door, I thought, and I might get nostalgic about English Soil.

Five minutes later, the large, old-fashioned door opened into the main body of the embassy. An official appeared, made for the front door and closed it. It clicked shut, the daylight disappeared. I didn't have time to muse about any possible transportation to Moscow inside a diplomatic bag. The smartly dressed man came straight over to me and asked if he could be of help. I was in my sober suit, having left the boiler suit at home on this occasion. The man spoke courteously, introducing himself as Sergei Lavrov, the Second Secretary. I gave him my visiting card with my name ('Rev. Dr') and address and phone number, though I wondered if this was a wise move. I explained that I was a priest and an orthopaedic surgeon and that I had spent six weeks recently in a cell in a church in Birmingham to draw attention to the plight of Irina Ratushinskaya. I reminded him that she was a Christian poetess in prison in the Soviet Union because of her poetry and that she was now very ill.

'I am worried about her because she has been refused medical treatment,' I said. I sought to reassure him that I was not anti-Soviet but simply concerned for the girl and her safety. He took my literature. It included examples of Irina's poetry, and a request for members of the public to write to the Soviet Embassy, and details of Irina's story.

To his credit, he listened, and we talked together for some forty minutes. I felt that, as I described Irina's circumstances and various illnesses, we made personal contact. I looked him in the eye. When I got to the bit about the punishment cell, the cold, and the rags, his eyes narrowed ever so slightly before he regained his composure and gave the official Soviet reply. I'm not sure, but I think he felt for her. Of course, he said: that a priest shouldn't meddle in politics; that she was a criminal and was getting her just deserts and haven't we got sick people in our prisons, too? They were all the right answers, of course, but I felt that it didn't have much heart in it. I told him about my family, invited him for tea at my house, and after a prayer, I left, assuring him of my thanks and emphasizing my desire to see Irina freed and my good will towards this nation. As I reached the door, he opened it for me. We exchanged our goodbyes. I thought I'd just check that I had everything. Glancing over at the settee, I saw my slim black pocket diary lying there, ready to slither down the back and out of sight. I excused myself and went over to pick it up. It was only as I turned out of the avenue on to Bayswater Road that my heart missed a few beats at the thought of how near a miss that had been. The diary had lots of names and addresses which I'd rather not feed into their computer.

The security man on the gate at King Charles Street pointed across the central courtyard of the Foreign Office to the large doors by which I could enter to see Mr Renton. Weaving in and out of the parked cars, I made my way diagonally across the imposing square from which the Empire had been governed. Mr Renton's staff came to meet me. Andy Henderson escorted me up the grand staircase, the walls around which were lined with portraits of yesterday's eminent statesmen. I could picture the occasional Viceroy of India mounting by the same carpeted stair.

The 'team' ushered me into the spacious and elegantly appointed ministerial office. Mr Renton rose from his desk

115

which looked out on to a view of Horseguards Parade and St James's Park.

The Minister greeted me warmly. I thanked him for seeing me and for his help so far. I think he was a bit taken aback. I got the impression that members of the public don't always start with thanks! Miss Fisher was there from the Soviet Department. I knew her name as a signatory of some of the letters I'd had sent on to me. The Minister kindly asked after my health and I explained that a bit of home cooking and a few Easter eggs had taken care of that long ago. He said how much parliamentary concern there had been over Irina and that he'd had a tremendous amount of correspondence about her. I apologized for his extra work.

He let me spell out clearly what had prompted me to support Irina and expose the horrors of the camps, while at the same time not seeking to be anti-Soviet. He accepted a copy of Irina's poems in the David McDuff translation and subsequently, I noticed, read from her poetry on the floor of the House of Commons. We discussed the Soviet Foreign Minister's visit in July and I asked whether Irina could be mentioned on that occasion by someone who mattered and who was sympathetic to her plight. He couldn't make any promises but confirmed that they were certainly very concerned about her, and that Lord Whitelaw's delegation *had* included her name in the list which they gave to Mr Gorbachev.

I told them of my visit to the Soviet Embassy earlier that afternoon and they agreed it was very unusual for a passer-by to get straight in to talk to a diplomat of considerable seniority.

It was a useful visit. He and his staff were willing to help as much as they could. It was up to me to keep demonstrating that there was public concern.

'The more of a fuss you make of someone like Irina,' he said, 'the more value it gives that person in the eyes of the Soviet Government as a bargaining counter in the arena of international relations.'

I left feeling Mr Renton was willing. And we were not just posturing. I wanted to provide evidence to enable our leaders to go to the Soviet leaders and say, 'Please, if you want to respect our concerns give some attention to clearing up this appalling aspect of Soviet life.'

The matter was still urgent. Irina's blood pressure was so high that she could easily have suffered a stroke or a coronary—if the readings were accurate. The periods of loss of consciousness in her cell were worrying. If the pressure was that great, it would be a lot of work for the heart to get up sufficient pressure even to open the valve out of the heart into the aorta in order to start pumping blood round the body. If that started to fail, she'd have heart failure and be in big trouble very quickly. The deliberate act of withholding adequate medical treatment seemed very callous.

Back home, we got ready for the nation-wide Vigil. Some fifty or so places around the British Isles were going to do something special on the last weekend in June. Some were getting together petitions.

A man in Kent had a stall at a fair. Margaret Hunter in Royston, near Cambridge, got into a wooden cage and the whole village came and looked at the spectacle. Dorothy Regan in Nottingham made a cage. Her daughters, the Mayor, a bishop or two, and all sorts of people also got mixed up in it one way or another. Similar events happened at Wells, Plymouth, Edinburgh, East Grinstead, Birmingham, Oundle and elsewhere.

I prepared for a press conference on the previous Friday. In my struggle to procure some continental coverage, I got Italian, French, German and Spanish translations of a statement which I was going to practise and then read to the television stations of all these countries. I traced a map of Britain and put a spot on it in every place where some event was happening. I was hoping that if the media tested it out, I'd be able to match each spot with something actually taking place.

The peripheral bits of my map didn't have many spots, so I got on the phone to my Methodist friend in Lerwick, Shetland who agreed to do something. She didn't know what they would do, but it would be enough to deserve another spot on my map!

I got on to people in Belfast, Aberdeen, Inverness, Exeter, Plymouth and Truro. It all made enough to call the whole operation a 'National Vigil'. It even included events at John O'Groats and Land's End.

I then set about making an enormous banner of Irina. We had an intensely black-and-white silhouette photo of Irina which I had made into a slide. (It appears on the cover of this book.) I projected it on to a large cotton sheet, traced the outline of her face and then painted in the black bits with some 'textile ink'. The result was startling. It could be seen half a mile away, and the funny thing was that the further away you got the clearer her face became. I made a big frame to pin it on to, dismantled the timbers and went to bed early before getting the morning coach down to London for a press conference at St Bride's church, Fleet Street.

I never made it. Early in the morning, I found Sue writing a letter to her mum in the bathroom. 'I've started going into labour, Dick.'

'Oh no,' I thought. 'Not when I've got this press conference in London to go to.'

I pondered. Perhaps I could get the early bus back. It wasn't any good. I got on the phone.

'I'm terribly sorry, I can't come. Sue's in labour. Can you go ahead with the press conference without me?'

Alarmed and crestfallen, my organizer friend agreed. To calm him down, I said I'd get everything to him if he met the coach the other end at Victoria Coach Station.

Sue looked as if she'd be okay for an hour or so, so I got in the car and went down to the coach station. The driver looked at my ticket, believed my unlikely story and accepted the banner, along with all the other bits and pieces. However, he balked at the eight-foot timber beams needed to erect the banner.

'That's freight,' he declared abruptly. 'That's not going to London.'

Non-plussed, I settled for what he was prepared to take and cleared off home to Sue, feeling like a character out of a Brian Rix comedy.

I didn't know it at the time but someone else was at that very moment also getting ready to set out on a journey of some consequence.

The pain stopped! Sue spent most of the day doing the ironing and sorting out letters. I got on with writing letters. In the evening the pains restarted. We left Christopher with a friend and went to the hospital. Sue was a bit disgruntled when I went off to make some phone calls—one about Irina and the others to alert the family to the new developments.

At half-past midnight the agonies were over. I had to catch the baby's head as he plopped out. Sue relaxed waiting for the doctor to come in and see to her, as I played with our new addition to the family. He was really lovely, in perfect health with a smashing virile yawn.

Christopher came with me the next day to see his mum and 'tiny Tim'. All was well. He was no longer covered with blood. His head was no longer squashed out of shape. He was a really handsome little chap—and still is.

8

FIRST GLIMMERS OF PROGRESS

The 'National Vigil' generated a petition with some 11,000 signatures. Mr Shevardnadze, the Soviet Foreign Minister, was visiting London on 14 July, so we decided to try to hand in the petition at the Soviet Embassy during his visit. We didn't manage to find out his programme, just that he would be in Britain from the Sunday until the Tuesday.

Early on Monday morning, two dozen of us got on a hired coach outside the Edgbaston Cricket Ground and headed for London. The coach dropped us on Bayswater Road right opposite the Soviet Consulate. My parents were there with my nephews Peter and Tommy. Others had converged from Bath, Plymouth, Sussex and all over London. Fifty of us lined up opposite the Consulate behind crowd-control barriers and in front of a pub. The Afghan Mujahedeen were there before us. We erected our banners of Irina's face, two huge white sheets and four smaller ones. I put on my black cassock over my clerical shirt and dog collar.

Some read Irina's poems over the loud hailer. We sang hymns and prayed for Irina's release, kneeling on the pavement. It wasn't just an appearance of praying, we did really pray. TV crews from the BBC and two American companies were there. The police allowed two of us to go over to the gate of the Consulate which they said was the place for handing in petitions. Jackie and I went, armed with the big file of petition papers. I stood at the gate in my cassock and pressed the button on the intercom. It cracked and emitted a monosyllabic grunt by way of reply. After saying that I had a petition about Irina Ratushinskaya and would like to present it to the Embassy, there was silence—not even a monosyllabic grunt. So I continued. I explained who I was, who Irina was and about her conditions, emphasizing her blood pressure and lack of treatment. This approach produced results. The reply came back that the Consulate was closed.

It usually closes at 12.30 p.m. but it was only noon, which I drew to their attention. No reply. Unabashed I gave them a little bit for the tape recorders about international friendship and our desire for healthy relations but that 'the horrors of the gulag must stop'. I talked to Mr Gorbachev, Mr Shevardnadze, and if I'd thought, would have added a message for Mr Gromyko as well.

The police kindly suggested that we try the main embassy building. Followed by the TV crews, Jackie and I went along to the grand entrance lodge at the north end of the private avenue where the embassies are situated. The TV men could not follow past the lodge. This was no more successful, although various members of the embassy staff and their families did come up while we stood at the gate. They wouldn't enter into conversation about Irina. The intercom wasn't any more chatty than at the Consulate. We returned to the banners and our friends and supporters. We'd have to post the petition. The TV crews recorded our efforts and we dispersed, arranging to meet back at the bus for the home trip.

A handful of us went off into the adjacent corner of Hyde Park. As we sat nibbling our lunch, I noticed that we were near to a playing field which lay between Hyde Park proper and the backs of the embassies. It was 14 July and the French were out in the garden having a garden party to celebrate the Storming of the Bastille. There was a bit of activity on the far side of the football pitch. An ambulance and some police cars were parked there and a few men were wandering around rather aimlessly.

A smart, gleaming executive helicopter rattled over the tall green trees of the park. It touched down on the centre of the pitch. The rotors carried on for a few moments and then all was quiet.

We pressed up against the railings around the pitch as a line of policemen looked at us from the touch line. A Soviet ZIL limousine drove up to the helicopter. Figures disembarked. I thought it was Mr Shevardnadze but I wasn't sure. A voice near me shouted, 'Go home you filthy Russian swine', but readily conceded that it wasn't quite the image we wanted to portray and agreed not to do it again. I rehearsed in my mind the words Sue had taught me that morning and then shouted,

'Pahzhalsta, Pahzhalsta, Tavarishch Shevardnadze, Asvabadeetye Irinu Ratushinskuyu.' ('Please, please, Mr Shevardnadze, release Irina Ratushinskaya.')

I called out again and again. I think he heard. I'm not so sure whether the French garden party guests did, but some of them waved approvingly when I called out the French equivalent.

The cavalcade swept off and disappeared round the southern end of the row of embassies, evidently to take the distinguished visitor to the front entrance of the main embassy building. A couple of us beetled round to the front, past the entrance lodge. All but one of our banners and the petition were locked up in the coach, so we couldn't get at them.

We arrived outside the embassy to find a cavalcade of British police motor-cyclists forming up outside the gate ready to escort Mr Shevardnadze to Downing Street. The police didn't like people lingering here. We needed something to do to pass the time, while making sure that we didn't miss the Soviet Foreign Minister's party as they came out of the building and into the waiting limousines.

Fortunately, a woman called Marjorie was at the embassy gate with a plastic bag containing a greetings card and a little New Testament in Russian as a gift for Mr Shevardnadze. I'd never met her before. She introduced herself and explained that she'd been coming there for years, always with the same gentle message of peace and love. A rather older diplomat approached the gate from the other Soviet building opposite, and the lock buzzed in the gate releasing the catch. Marjorie and I engaged him in conversation. She was full of goodwill and comfort and asked that the packet be given to Mr Shevardnadze. Mr Yuro Mazur confirmed that he knew Marjorie and said that they were always pleased to see her. He took the packet and agreed to do what he could. He wasn't so keen to discuss

122

with me the case of Irina Ratushinskaya. He pushed the gate and walked up to the embassy door which opened to receive him. Marjorie knew I was from the demo in the morning and begged me not to shout or do anything silly. She felt it would destroy the goodwill she'd built up over the years. I felt a bit ashamed but mumbled a non-committal reply.

The doors opened and a group of dark-suited men came out on to the main steps some twenty yards away. I chanted my plea in Russian again, singing it out like a rag-and-bone man or, if you prefer, like an Anglican vicar at Morning Prayer. I reckoned it would carry better like that without sounding belligerent. There was no doubt that they'd heard loud and clear. It was so close, the road was very quiet and there was no wind. The quiet purr of the police motor-cycles would not have interrupted my plea.

'Please, please, Mr Shevardnadze, release Irina Ratushinskaya.' The group on the steps shuffled a bit. Faces looked over in my direction. I didn't notice what happened to Marjorie. I suspect she made herself scarce. The diplomats seemed to make a positive effort not to notice as Mr Shevardnadze continued to shake everybody's hand before taking his leave and getting into his limousine.

A big, burly sergeant rushed up to me.

'You ought to be ashamed of yourself! That's the sort of thing that football hooligans do!' (Though, of course, they don't usually do it in Russian!) I did notice, however, that he waited a few seconds before he rushed up to me and gave me plenty of time to call out my plea three times in Russian and once in English. He put me in the charge of a young constable whom he detailed to march me down to the gate lodge and out on to the street. No one laid a hand on me and it was all done in a courteous manner. Ten paces along the avenue, the young policeman spoke to me clearly but without turning his head and hardly moving his teeth:

'Smashing! That was great!'

All this took place without our knowing anything of Mr Shevardnadze's itinerary. It was about the most effective contact we could possibly have had with him and the timing was brilliant!

Three of us jumped into a car and headed off down to Downing Street with the one big banner we still had. Downing Street itself was blocked off. The adjacent pavement of Whitehall was choc-a-bloc first with the 'Thirty-Fives', the Women's Campaign for Soviet Jewry, and then the Afghan Mujahedeen. It was great to be able to get on with them all. Our common purpose allowed us to get together at the end of the day for a happy group photo of members of all three groups together, sporting our respective banners.

The choice was to take up a position further down the street after the Thirty-Fives and the Afghans had gone across to the other side of the street. We discussed it with the police on the Downing Street barrier who said,

'They don't let you stay over there for long.'

Technically, they didn't forbid us to go over there. So we got our double sheet ready the right way up, without making it too obvious, scrumpled it up again and stuffed it behind a low parapet on the edge of the Ministry of Defence lawn. We didn't want to spoil the effect of its suddenly being unfurled by having it the wrong way up!

We got a message through to the people who were by then keeping the rendezvous with the coach, and thanks to the driver's good nature, all came down to join in. They lined up with the Afghans displaying the other banners. Mr Shevardnadze was inside Number Ten all this time talking to Mrs Thatcher. After a few false alarms, the cavalcade was on the move again. As it swept out of Downing Street into Whitehall and off towards Nelson's Column, Jackie was stuck on the side of the street and felt she had to make a dash for it to help with unfurling the big banner. She got inadvertently caught up amongst the motor bikes and ended up running along the side of Mr Shevardnadze's car, purely by accident. Once there, however, she didn't lose the opportunity to point to the banners of Irina opposite. Mr Shevardnadze was seen to look over in their direction. The police took Jackie's name and address but no action was taken against her. It worried me a bit because we didn't intend any sort of civil disobedience. On the other hand, we are entitled in this country to non-violent demonstrations of this kind; guileless gestures which are not intended to harm anyone.

What became of the big banner? Just as the cavalcade was turning out of Downing Street, a tourist bus pulled across the front of us. The driver stopped to let his passengers have a good look up Downing Street in order to see the visiting dignitary. We had to do a bit of quick thinking, scrumpled up the banner again and nipped through the traffic jam which had formed, unfurling the banner some thirty feet, or less, from Mr Shevardnadze. He saw it okay! We didn't block the traffic and complied immediately with a policeman's order to clear the bus lane.

I flopped back into my seat in the coach, head pounding with a migraine. I hung my head right back to get some relief and nearly vomited. My head was about to burst but somehow, as never before, I didn't care. It had been a terrific day. Everybody had been great—not least the bus driver and the Metropolitan Police who, considering their duty to protect this visiting dignitary, were very accommodating—and the timing of everything was divine.

Later we discovered how the day had gone from the inside. It turned out that the helicopter had brought Mr Shevardnadze from the official country residence of Sir Geoffrey Howe, the Foreign Secretary. He had pressed the point about Irina. Tim Renton had done a good job and it sounded as if there was some pretty plain talking.

Our performance at the Embassy came his way, and when the poor man went to Downing Street, Mrs Thatcher told him of her concern about Irina as well. Apparently, he enjoyed his visit but the 'human-rights' issue got him a bit rattled.

In retrospect, I feel the most effective recipe in this sort of campaign is for the word to be spoken privately by our representatives at the right time into the right ear, backed up by a public expression of concern. That way, the two elements, private and public, endorse each other. It is also important to realize that some people can do one and not the other, and one should not push the mouth that's going to speak in private to disclose itself in public if it doesn't feel happy to do so.

Within days we had news—Irina was out of the prison camp. She had been taken from the camp back to her home city of Kiev. Officials in the camp came to her at the end of June and told her she was going to be released. She prepared for the event with customary reserve and knew she must not count her chickens before they were hatched. She gave her belongings—some extra clothing and a few oddments—to her friends.

They took her in a wagon to the civilian airport in the city of Saransk, some forty miles away. They led her on board a civilian airliner and sat her down in an airline seat with a guard on either side. The row behind was filled with prison guards or KGB personnel. She was segregated from the other passengers but not handcuffed. The air hostess on these flights usually brings round bottles of mineral water, but turned her eyes away when she got to Irina.

On reaching Kiev the passengers disembarked, along with Irina and her official companions. They all boarded the same air-side coach together, and disembarked at the civilian-passenger terminal building. The uniformed escort formed a cordon round the slim figure as they made their way through the crowd, the passive civilian passengers falling back on seeing the official escort.

I find it an amazing juxtaposition of two worlds. I think British tourists use that same airport building. Had you been there, you'd have seen Irina escorted out of the terminal concourse. No need to wait at the baggage claim. She still had her bald shaven head, her sunken cheeks, her legs like sticks and her prison clothes.

She arrived back at the same wooden prison on Vladimirskaya Street. They told her she was free and could go. She just had to jot down a brief appeal for clemency and she could go home to be with Igor. They would even give her a lift. The problem was that Irina had no intention of ever appealing for clemency. She wrote no such appeal. She signed nothing—and they didn't release her. She noticed, however, that the food improved. Try as he might, Igor was granted no visit.

Keston published the news of her transfer, but the feeling was that it would only be for a brief period of re-education, an attempt to soften her up and get her to recant. By all accounts, it sounded unlikely that she was the sort that would oblige and she'd be back in the camp before long, as had happened to Raisa Rudenko. There was some hesitation at Keston about publicizing her new temporary prison address. She'd be there such a short time that it would only confuse people writing to her at the new address.

I wasn't so sure about it being temporary. While she was there, we had a chance of keeping her out of camp. It would be easier to release her from there than after her return to the camp. We had to get cracking and make the most of it.

They wouldn't let Igor meet his wife, although they did let him leave a parcel for her. You have to be careful what you put in these parcels. They allow margarine but not butter. The KGB keep a cat at Vladimirskaya Street which sniffs the parcels and can tell the difference!

The Bolshoi Ballet came and we were there to meet them—or at least to meet the audience as it arrived for the opening night. Having liaised with the 'house manager' and the police, we gathered once more on the pavement, opposite the main entrance to the Covent Garden Opera House. I got there very early and was allotted a length of crowd-control barrier. Mum and Dad came down from North London with the banners which they had kindly stored for us, and my sister Mary with Paddy and his brothers formed the advance party, while another supporter went off round the newspaper offices to let them know. Our banner in Russian and English said, 'Welcome Bolshoi but let IRINA go!'

We had had a new batch of postcards printed for the audience to take and send to the Soviet Ambassador. They referred to Irina's move to Kiev and begged once more for her release. They included a note of the address of our Vigil Office and bore Irina's picture on the reverse.

The Jewish campaigners arrived and set up their banners followed by the Afghans who were allotted the next bit of barrier further down the street.

As the audience gathered, we positioned supporters to hand out our cards at all the entrances and nearly everybody, including the management, took it in good spirits. A lot of the audience had heard of Irina on the arts programme

Kaleidoscope on BBC Radio 4. The house manager came out and accepted a card which he promised to give to the Political Supervisor of the Ballet Company. He was eager to do this to avert any desire by campaigning groups to get into the auditorium and make a fuss. I gather that one night another group did so but this was nothing to do with us. An Opera House official gave out an announcement each night, asking people not to disrupt the performance by staging any protest inside the auditorium during the evening. Each night his plea was greeted by cheers from the audience. I think the object of the exercise was not directly to address any would-be protestors, but to let them see that a disruptive demo was likely to be counter-productive as a public relations exercise!

The '35's' Jewish group started chanting as the people arrived in their dinner jackets and evening dresses with fur stoles. They were mostly on foot but some came in chauffeur-driven limousines. Being the 'gala night' with the Princess of Wales present, there were a fair number of these. The '35's' shouted:

All One! two! three! four!
Open up the Iron Door!
Five! six! seven! eight!
Let our people emigrate!
Cheerleader What do we want?
All Freedom!
Cheerleader When do we want it?
All Now!

They repeated this again and again. It was brilliantly effective.

In the gaps we sang 'Praise my soul, the King of Heaven' from the *Hymns Ancient and Modern Revised*. It didn't have quite the same 'umph' to it, I must admit. We tacitly accepted that we couldn't compete with our colleagues and didn't really want to, so we gave up singing!

Our banners were effective, though. The police commented that they were really eye catching even from the other end of Bow Street.

A limousine with a red flag on the bonnet arrived. The chanting became a roar. The occupant didn't waste much time heading for the theatre door. The latecomers straggled to the entrance and nothing happened for a bit. A policeman actually signed one of our postcards! And his boss came and said it had been good 'working with you!'

Then, with a whoosh, a couple of Rovers swept into the little street from our end, the opposite way from most of the traffic. They pulled up sharply at the theatre door. The doors of the second car exploded open and half-a-dozen business-like men with bulging arm pits erupted on to the street, advancing in an ever-enlarging concentric circle around the front car. They stared at the crowd and the windows and roof tops of the surrounding buildings, taking the evening air.

The door of the white Rover in front was opened from outside and an elegant figure in a glittering evening dress and a tiara stepped out and disappeared in through the doors. With a quick glance round at the crowd, we saw the face of the Princess of Wales. It was quite a thrill for the kids and made up for a rather tedious afternoon.

We followed the Bolshoi throughout its tour of Britain, different groups concentrating on different cities.

After all that, a holiday was in order. Nearly the whole extended family went off for a week to Charmouth on the Dorset coast for our annual family holiday. As we approached the cottage, Paddy, my sister's nine-year-old, stumbled and staggered back towards me losing his balance. He hadn't tripped on anything; he'd just lost his balance. I realized that something was wrong that needed sorting out. It sounded like his cerebellum, the part of the brain that helps you to balance.

Whilst we were on holiday the following week with my cousin in Norfolk, Paddy was admitted to the Children's Hospital where tests were done. Mum and Dad rang to tell us what had happened and that the doctors were worried he might have a brain tumour. He was having a CT scan that morning. I rang Mary. We piled all our gear into the car and left forthwith with apologies to our hosts.

Pulling up at the kerb outside the Children's Hospital, we were just in time to see Mary coming down the steps. The other boys were restless and wanted to get away to get some ice cream. Mary looked in a dream. She pursed her lips wist-

129

fully. 'It's true Paddy does have a brain tumour—a great big one in the cerebellum. He'll have to be operated on tomorrow.'

They warned Mary and Anthony that he might not pull through. He looked very wan and sickly and was never far off vomiting. On the day of the operation we brought him a present of his favourite Medieval Lego to try and focus his mind. I anointed him with oil and we prayed that Jesus would look after him. It was ordinary cooking oil from the kitchen at home, the stuff we fry eggs in, but it didn't matter. What did matter was that our prayers would be answered and that Paddy would recover. He didn't die on the operating table, but he looked terrible even on the Saturday evening. The surgeon said that it's at forty-eight hours post-op that you can see how he's going to be——whether or not he'll recover consciousness. By Saturday evening, things looked really bad. On Sunday morning he was drinking a bit. During the week, he gradually woke up. He did well and by the end of the week they allowed him to go home.

He couldn't see well and it turned out that the pressure in his head had damaged the optic nerves. Eventually, he lost his sight completely and has not recovered it. A month later he became paraplegic from further trouble down the spine. He could hardly move his legs. Mercifully, this recovered well after radiotherapy, anti-tumour drugs and lots of people's prayers. Eight months later, he's making good progress typing away on his Braille typewriter at a handicapped school almost next door to our house. And he mastered the medieval Lego ages ago!

More news came of Irina. Her mother had been allowed a meeting with her in July. Then in early August Igor heard from her over the phone in his flat. She was speaking from prison. If he came round the next day, she told him, the prison authorities would grant a meeting.

Needless to say, he was overjoyed. The guards were quite civil towards him. Irina and Igor were allowed to meet at last, although they had to sit at opposite sides of a table, with a guard watching to ensure that they didn't touch each other or pass anything. No news could be exchanged of campaigns in the West. She seemed in good heart but was pale and weak and getting lots of attacks of severe chest pain.

These meetings with relatives vary a lot. One Baptist guitarist, Valeri Barinov, was visited by his family at a camp in the far north. They were only allowed to see him through a glass screen and had to shout to make themselves heard. There were several other families in the visitors' half of the room, all trying to shout to their loved ones through the same glass screen, so the whole scene was a noisy pandemonium. The family of Anna Chertkova, a Baptist, wrongfully detained in a psychiatric hospital, last saw her in Tashkent, in a room divided similarly by a glass screen. They were only allowed to talk on a telephone. At the other end of the scale, 'long visits' are sometimes granted, during which the visiting wife or husband can be locked into a special visitors' shed together with their spouse where they are left alone by the guards.

The authorities tried to get her family and friends to persuade her to sign an appeal for clemency, but to no avail. Then they said that they understood her reticence, but if her relatives signed on her behalf, without referring to her, then everybody would be happy. She would not have compromised herself because the family would have done everything for her, and the authorities would have their piece of paper.

Irina was having none of that. She had seen this sort of thing before. The authorities would make every bit of mileage possible out of her appeal, and it would come over as her having recanted. She had done nothing wrong. She had nothing to apologize for. Clemency or forgiveness was not appropriate; to appeal for clemency would be to acknowledge her guilt and to recant.

She didn't sign. The KGB know how to exploit any apparent 'recantation' to the full. Several prisoners who have eventually been broken down, have appeared on prime-time television and offered abject apologies for their 'over-inflated ideas' and the 'despicable actions' resulting from them. For instance, Father Dimitri Dudko, a saintly and effective parish priest from the Moscow region, was arrested and held incommunicado for six months, while he was in the hands of the KGB. Then one day he appeared on television and gave a long apology. Throughout the broadcast he sat with an inappropriate vague smile on his face and appeared to be behaving in a manner quite unlike his usual self. Then the next day he was released.

Of course, to Irina the need to resist unwanted propositions from the authorities was nothing new. Ever since school and certainly since the year 1972 when the KGB had failed to recruit her at university, she had learned how to resist persuasion. They wouldn't have been very pleased at her refusal on either occasion, especially when she refused to be implicated in the anti-Semitic exam arrangements at the teacher training college. Irina had learnt how to stand her ground.

Several prisoners in the recent releases have chosen to resist the invitation to sign an appeal and an agreement in order to walk free from prison. Some have been released anyway, or the agreement has been altered to make it a bland general approval of the policy of *Glasnost* (openness). In other cases, the prisoners have been sent back to the camps even when they were on the verge of freedom. Irina risked going back to Barashevo and the 'small zone', but she stuck to her guns. If they did send her back, it wouldn't be by plane. It would be by prison wagon on a slow prison train. These haven't been updated much since the days of *Dr Zhivago*. Bedding is minimal. The cold is biting and the food consists of dry hunks of bread and very little water. The women are allowed to go to the toilet only twice a day. Any more than that and you have to batter on the side of the truck until they take you out. The transit prisons are appalling. You are usually kept here while waiting for a connection with a prison train on the next lap of your journey. Some have described water flowing across the floor, underground cells, walls covered in blood-speckled tuberculotic sputum, cells full of steam or covered in ice. The journeys often take a very long time. There's no comparison with civilian travelling times. A month for a train journey in these conditions would not be unusual. It is obviously a calculated part of the suffering. The Soviet high-ups were undoubtedly getting eager to get rid of Irina.

We had to step up our efforts to secure her release. We

planned to mark the fourth anniversary of her arrest, 17 September, by poetry readings or other events in as many places as we could. The Poetry Society organized the central event very well indeed. It took place at St James's Church, Piccadilly, in the centre of London's West End. We had already sent out letters to people, inviting them to do something in their own areas and many of the people who did something at the end of June did so again.

By this time, Irina's poetry was available not only in Russian and English but also in French, Polish, German, Norwegian and Dutch. I wrote round to all the people I could think of and a lot of contacts given me at second hand—some 400 letters in all. It spread out the event pretty well. Poetry readings were held, I understand, in Chicago, Denver, New York, Oslo, Bonn, Milan, Melbourne and in New Zealand. Not all were at our initiative. The United States ones were organized by Yefim Kotlyar, Irina's friend in Chicago, and other campaigners.

The pace quickened, and in late August more news arrived. The couple had had a second meeting. This time they were allowed to sit together on the same bench. The guard sat unobtrusively in the far corner of the interview room and did not intervene for two hours. Igor put his arm round his wife for the first time in three years. He said, 'I don't know what they are up to but it's lovely while it lasts!'

Even more bizarre, the KGB put Irina in a car and drove her round the sights of Kiev, to whet her appetite for freedom. They took her to Igor's factory where he worked as a fitter. As they sat in the car, they pointed out to her the very window behind which Igor would be working.

'Sign,' they said, 'and you will be home with him within minutes, we'll see to it.'

'Sign,' she thought, 'and I'll be one of the living dead.'

9

TO THE SUMMIT

I didn't even know how to spell it: Reykjavik. I got the car out and took myself off up to Universal Travel, the shop on the corner in Northfield, near our home. I think the girls in there thought it was a bit out of the ordinary—Reykjavik! I wouldn't have been surprised if they'd asked me to step to one side and let them get on with some proper work, like a package holiday to Torremolinos. However, they did at least look up the price— £240. I wavered, obviously for too long. They checked it again and all the £240 seats had gone. It had to be Club Class at £420.

Crestfallen, I thanked them very much and slunk out of the door back to the car. There wasn't any point in considering it. I'd recovered slightly by the time I got home. Sue looked very relieved. Yet another hare-brained scheme had been shelved! I read the paper again and had a think and a pray. President Reagan and First Secretary Gorbachev were going to meet in Iceland to discuss arms control. All the world's press would be there. No! I had to go. It didn't matter about the cash. It would sort itself out. I couldn't let this opportunity go by. This is what it was all about. I must be there to represent Irina's interests when the 'big boys' meet. I didn't exactly know what I'd do. I might end up wandering the streets with my hands in my pockets, but I couldn't do anything if I didn't get there in the first place. There would obviously be a mad rush for seats on the flights for Reykjavik, in fact the media people made block bookings as soon as they heard and thought about who to fill them with later!

Back up at the travel agents the women were a bit taken aback to see me again, even more so when I made a firm booking and came back fifteen minutes later with a banker's cheque for £420. I told them what it was all about and they had the grace to wish me all the best. It turned out that we had a bit more in the bank than usual. I obviously needed somewhere to stay, not that I was very bothered. I could always camp, even if it meant a long walk. The one o'clock news announced that the Icelandic government were not letting people off the plane without evidence of pre-arranged accommodation. Two thousand five hundred newsmen and diplomats were trying to squash into Reykjavik's 800 guest beds. My £420 and the whole effort looked like going down the drain. I rang Ron Newby, the Children's Society organizer whom I'd just met at a conference and who'd invited me over to his house the following week. I rang to say I couldn't come and explained why.

'Oh!' he said, 'you must look up the daughter of some friends of ours. She's English and he's Icelandic, an accountant at the Keflavik NATO Base. I'm sure they'd like to see you.'

I rang Ron's friends in Leamington Spa. They were very excited and offered to ring their daughter that evening to fix something up for me. I did gather, though, that the NATO base is some thirty miles out of Reykjavik and although a bit of floor space at their home would be most welcome, I might still get caught inside the military zone and not be allowed into the capital at a sensitive time like a summit conference. I had to find somewhere in Reykjavik, even if it was the camp site.

My sister Sue had a friend at medical school who was half Italian and half Icelandic, Betsy Fumagali, though when I contacted her, Sue was pretty gloomy about the chances of finding her friend. It was ten years since they'd last been in touch. Sue knew that Betsy practised under her maiden name which she couldn't remember, so the medical directory would be no use. But then a few minutes later the phone rang. Sue had rung Mum and Dad who had found a number for Betsy in their visitors book. It was quite old and I thought it would probably be little use. However, when I finally got through, she was there, and remembered who I was and did still have relatives in Iceland! Her cousin lived in Hafnarfjurdur on the outskirts of Reykjavik. Then

135

she remembered that her cousin Agnethe's mother-in-law ran the Salvation Army hostel right in the city centre, an ideal place, if there was a bed, but what with all the news-men wanting rooms, there was little hope that they'd still have one.

When I rang back the following evening, Betsy was jubilant. Oscar and Inma at the Salvation Army found that they had overlooked a room when the TV company man called to reserve rooms en bloc. They had a double room left which they hadn't given to him. I could have it and it was only a hundred yards away from the Soviet Embassy, right in the city centre. I was very conscious that God was in all this and arranging things better than any travel agent.

I went to a clergy meeting in Birmingham. The chairman let me tell everybody I was off to Reykjavik—I couldn't contain my excitement. One of them had spent a holiday touring Iceland the previous year and lent me all sorts of maps and guides. I was also given a marvellous epic poem of 'The Passion Psalmir', the Passion of Christ, by Hallgrimmur Petersson, the ancient forefather of the Ice-landic church, which, so I'm told, every Icelander is brought up on. It looked a useful means of identifying with any Icelandic Christians whom I might meet and wanted to co-operate with. I took it gladly.

I wanted to make sure that when I got to Iceland, I could get to see someone with reasonable seniority on both the American and Russian sides. I also felt I might engage in some sort of act of solidarity with Irina, like the cage, for which I'd have to get the support of the Icelandic Christians —I couldn't do it my own. It was a bit of a tall order trying to raise a team of supporters in Iceland while sitting at my desk in Birmingham, but I thought I'd have a go. Directory Enquiries put me on to the Icelandic Tourist Bureau, who told me the number for the Bishop of Iceland. The line was terribly crackly, but he agreed to meet me when I arrived. It was not the place to discuss a campaign in detail over the phone.

I would need introductions. David, my vicar, gave me a letter on the parish's headed notepaper to say I came with the support of the St David's congregation. I obviously had to tackle the Bishop who had seemed a bit reluctant during the pre-Christmas period and during the 'caged Vigil'. I explained where I was going and he got excited.

'Oh yes,' he enthused. 'What are you going to do, a demo?'

'Well, I wasn't going to put it quite as bluntly as that, but since you say so, yes I am!'

He wrote me letters of introduction to the Icelandic Bishop and to the Ambassadors of the United States and the Soviet Union in Reykjavik, saying that I was a priest in good standing in the diocese and that many people in Birmingham shared my concern over Irina.

I sent off telegrams to the relevant offices in Moscow and Washington. I managed to find a roving ambassador, Ambassador Jack Matlock, in Washington, who was going with the President, so I rang him and sent a telegram. A campaigning organization outside Washington got excited when I rang. Their director was going to meet the President the next day. He told him all about it.

Tim Renton's team at the Foreign Office helped a lot. Altogether, I did what I could to ensure that both groups of people, the Americans and the Russians, knew I was coming, and I hoped that the Russians would have a slight feeling of unease about my arrival. They might feel it would be worth their while to turn events to their own propaganda advantage and defuse the situation.

A British student Christian organization gave me the phone number of their Icelandic counterpart and I got through again, this time to Gudni Gunnarsson, their staff worker. He was a bit taken aback at first but asked me to get in touch when I arrived, as did Reykjavik Amnesty International.

The most important introduction of all came from less likely quarters. Paddy was back in hospital having his chemotherapy and felt pretty out of sorts. He'd turned out on loads of occasions to support me, so I asked Mary and Anthony whether it would be okay to get him to sign a greeting card to Reagan and one to Gorbachev as intro-ductions for me. They said okay. So I put it to Paddy and he leapt at the idea.

'Yes, rather! I'm tired of praying for Irina every day. I wish Mr Gorbachev would let her out!' Kids put it so beautifully!

So Paddy not only signed the cards, he wrote a greeting in each. It was the first thing he had written since going blind. He wrote very shakily, 'Please Mr Gorbachev let Irina go! Patrick' and 'Please President Reagan get Mr Gorbachev to let Irina go! Patrick'. It was very wobbly writing but you could make it out. I took the cards and wrote opposite Paddy's message an explanation as to his predicament and the fact that this was his first written message to anyone since the operation. They were precious cards. I wondered if it was all a bit below the belt, but I concluded that it wasn't. The whole exercise was to do with the tragedy of human suffering and Paddy's was as valid as anyone else's if it helped the superpower leader to see it all in personal terms. The 'Irina Vigil' Committee met and balked a bit at my abrupt, undemocratic action but eventually backed me up. I spent a night on duty at the Accident Hospital and the nurses had a whip round to raise some cash to help with the trip.

Amnesty International had arranged a service in the ruins of Coventry Cathedral and invited the 'man in the cage' to come and read something from the Bible in company with Jeremy Irons and others.

'You are Peter and on this rock I will build my church,' I called out. 'And the gates of hell shall not prevail against it!' The words felt as if they had a power all of their own.

There I met Canon Paul Oestreicher who is well known for his East-West peace work and who has earned the respect of many leaders in the East. He agreed to give me a letter of introduction. He had no headed notepaper so I had to collect it in London. His introduction would mean a lot to the Soviets.

In London the Jews gave me an introduction. They said it might not be very welcome, but we'd stand or fall together. Lambeth Palace also obliged. They not only put a letter in my hand, but did a lot of chasing round for me behind the scenes. I rang the bell at the medieval entrance to the Palace and entered up the grand flight of stairs to receive the envelope.

I brought a detailed map of Reykjavik. I always like to know where I am. I told the press, TV and radio that I was going, especially the BBC Russian service and the American Radio Free Europe. Even if it didn't achieve much, I reflected, the trip to Iceland certainly got the British media people excited. They suddenly seemed to take it all seriously and several wanted to cover it, and asked me to ring in a report when I was there.

One of the press people said, 'I should check your seat on the aeroplane if I were you. There seems to have been a bit of funny business and the bigger customers are pushing others out.'

'Yes,' I said, 'but I've got my ticket.'

'Doesn't count for anything, you'll be sorry! Okay, they might give a refund but that's not the point.'

Alarmed, I rang Icelandair. No, they couldn't find my name on the computer! How did I spell Rodgers? No, there was nothing.

Horrors! I got that strangulation feeling, and didn't know where to turn. I rang Universal Travel, my voice trembling a bit. After several phone calls, they finally found my name. I rang again half an hour later, spoke to a different operator and they'd still got my name. I was reassured. The *Church Times* had covered the Vigil well and seemed prepared to help. I called at their office and the Editor wrote me a 'To whom it may concern' letter appointing me as the correspondent to the *Church Times*, London, to cover the summit conference at Reykjavik with special reference to the case of Irina Ratushinskaya. With profuse thanks and the promise of an article, I tucked the letter away safely in my wallet.

I called on the Soviet Embassy, and had a good chat with the Soviet duty officer over the intercom, explaining what I was up to and that I was going to call at their Reykjavik embassy on Thursday and would they kindly arrange for me to be seen. I think the message reached its mark, even though the officer wasn't very chatty. I wanted to let them know I'd be at Reykjavik, just to let them worry slightly that there might be cause for a bit of embarrassment if Irina was not out in time, and to encourage them to maximize the propaganda benefit of releasing her.

I woke early on Wednesday, 8 October. Mum and Dad drove me down to the BBC in Portland Place to do a piece for *Woman's Hour*. They had followed Irina's case through pretty well and did use my interview. Then there was another introductory letter to be picked up. I was then dropped at South Kensington to get the tube out to London Airport. I got there in plenty of time, and checked in at the Icelandair desk.

'Oh, I'm sorry, sir. The flight's cancelled.' I must have looked a bit pale. The ticket seemed real enough. I expostulated, but nothing I could do could make her change her mind. The ground could have opened up and swallowed me. I felt really powerless.

I went off to ring the Icelandair office who had confirmed the flight and the seat a day or two before. It transpired after a while that it was a delay not a cancellation. The undercarriage had broken on landing at Keflavik. It would need repair and the aircraft wouldn't get to London in time to leave before 10 p.m. that night. They suggested I stand by for another flight which was just closing. I got my name on a list, having been bypassed by a queue of news men who sussed out the predicament quicker than I did. It was a rare scene—rare to me anyway. Cameramen and reporters were festooned everywhere. The enormous crates of TV equipment being taken as excess baggage must have cost as much as my fare, at least. The reporters all had handy little portable computers with pop-up screens which can connect to a phone and send the whole story straight down the wire to their newspaper's own computer. The *Church Times* Reykjavik correspondent with his ten-pence biro felt a bit of an amateur by comparison!

They called out the names of those queuing to go and stand by. I couldn't see the list and any glimpse I got was upside down anyway. With all these old hands my chances seemed slim. I didn't fancy making the right contacts at Keflavik at 1a.m. Suddenly they called out for Mr Rodgers and closed the flight. I was last on. With a quick call to bid

140

Sue farewell, I scrambled across the tarmac up the rear stairs of the DC9.

England dropped away on a grey gloomy afternoon. The visual impact of the flight was a non-event, nothing but cloud all the way. What I did see was more enlightening, a pleasant Icelandic couple on their way home from a holiday in England. He was a policeman. I quizzed him, and he told me what I wanted to know. The President of Iceland was a lady, Vigdis Finnbogadottir; the Prime Minister was Steingrimor Hermannsson; the Chief of Police, Bodvar Bragason; the Bishop of Iceland was Herra Biskup Petur Sigurgeirsson and the Mayor was David Oddsson. 'There are a lot of sons and daughters in Iceland,' I remarked. (In Iceland they add 'sson' for someone's son and 'dottir' for daughter.)

I mugged up lots of Icelandic expressions like 'Good morning' and 'Thank you' taught me by my flying companions, but then the engines changed pitch and the no-smoking lights came on. After a long descent, we finally emerged from the cloud base as buildings were whipping past, and we were down.

It was a gloomy place. The cloud hung low over the hangars. An AWACS (I think) stood on the tarmac and a Russian Ilyushin or two. Emerging from the rear door, the air was fresh and bracing and flavoured with kerosene. The blustery wind gusted through the shaggy, bedraggled grass. We made a bee-line for the slatted walk-way to the single-storey terminal. The NATO base is the only international airport for the island. It handles civilian as well as military traffic.

Apart from my case getting left in London, there were no problems. The Immigration Officer was very apologetic about the mess-up and offered to get me a toothbrush and shaving gear. The TV equipment had taken all the space in the hold. My accommodation arrangements satisfied immigration. The man ahead of me in the queue explained he was a civilian under contract to the US Navy. Once through immigration I met Hermann Bjarnarsson, who had turned out to give me a warm welcome. He packed me off on the bus to the capital and returned to his work having

arranged to pick me up in Reykjavik on Sunday evening.
He invited me to stay with him, which would be handy for
my flight home on the Monday.

The bus pulled out from the terminal car park and
made for the capital. Our bus pulled up at its city terminus,
the Loftleidir Hotel.

I wore my dog collar to identify myself in the crowd.
The sharp eyes of a youthful Nordic mother approached
me. She turned out to be Agnethe Kristiannsson who had
come to meet me on her way home from school. She taught
at a school in the suburbs at which Vigdis Finnbogadottir
had been a colleague of hers before entering politics and
becoming the President of Iceland.

We pulled out of the car park, splashing through the
puddles and made for the main road leading into the town.

'People don't stand on ceremony here,' Agnethe
explained, 'the very arrangement of names means that you
can't go and ask for Mr Oddsson or Mr Hermannsson. You
just ask for them by their christian name and father's name
—it's all a big family business. If you want to speak to the
President, you just go and ask for her in the same way.'

Agnethe took me across to the north side of the peninsula to see the clapboard house standing on a lawn next to
the rocky shore-line which was to be the meeting place for
the summit leaders. Screens were being erected in the
blustery evening light to block off the line of sight from
adjacent warehouses and offices to prevent sharp-eyed lip-
readers from eavesdropping. A few official-looking gents
were padding around on the grass, mumbling up their
sleeves as their coat tails flapped in the breeze.

The Salvation Army Hostel is a four-storey block just
off the main city square, a stone's throw from the 'Althing'
or parliament, and offering good simple hospitality. The
protective figures of Oscar and his wife, Inma, welcomed
us, and showed me up the staircase to my first-floor room.
The room was frugal, with a little wash basin in the corner,
a simple table, wardrobe, quilted bed and locker. It was
warm and I was fortunate to have it to myself.

Agnethe left me to it, and after a snack, I went out to
explore, calling on the Catholic priest, Father Hjalti

Thorkelson, and his new Irish curate whom I had met on the plane on the way over.

I told them why I had come. The idea didn't immediately fire them with enthusiasm, although they were interested and hospitable. Their Bishop was with them and was gravely ill at the time.

Back at the Salvation Army, I placed a row of coins in the groove on top of the coin box, dialled England and our number in Birmingham. Sue's cheery voice answered at the other end, while the kroners rolled and disappeared down the slot. It was a good line but it didn't last long. Everyone at home was fine.

I turned in. My room was warm and adequately heated. With an Icelandic duvet, it felt almost like a summer's evening in Spain. I spared a thought for the occupant of another room who I thought would be considerably colder.

It was fresh early the next morning when I got out and started to get my bearings. The centre of Reykjavik is very small. The city is set on a peninsula a mile wide by some three miles long, projecting westwards from the south-west coast of Iceland. The suburbs cluster round its base and at the seaward tip, but the main square with the parliament building and the Salvation Army hostel lies in a low gap running north-south between two gentle hills. On the western rise stands the Catholic church and further on, a large flat expanse which accommodates the Saga Hotel, the home of the visiting Soviet delegation, and the Hagaskoli or high school, which had been taken over as a press centre. At the base of this rise, not a hundred yards from my hostel, lies the Soviet Embassy, a four-storey house with a red flag and a lot of aerials. The eastward rise is surmounted by a modern church in concrete, its striking pinnacle the most notable landmark of the city, named after Hallgrimmur Petersson, the author of the epic Hymn of Christ's Passion of which my friend had lent me a copy. On the slope south towards the lakes and the airport are the United States and British Embassies situated amid a residential area of robust weatherproof houses.

Back at the hostel, Oscar offered me a lift to pick up

my suitcase which had arrived at the domestic airport. Then the British Ambassador was expecting me and was very helpful. He had arrived the day before, on the same plane as me. The Soviets hadn't replied but the Americans had someone who would be glad to see me. The diplomatic directory showed that the Soviet Ambassador in Reykjavik was Mr Evgeny Kosarev. Failing him, I should try to speak to Mr Vladimir Prosvirin.

At the Soviet Embassy, I opened the low gate and approached the heavy wooden door with its bullet-proof peep-hole. I buzzed the bell, the catch buzzed back at me and the door opened. I found myself in the tiny, darkened lobby with a plain-clothes guard looking at me through another bullet-proof screen. People were milling around up and down the stairs and squeezing past me in the confined space. It all seemed to be an unaccustomed bustle of activity in preparation for the arrival of the bosses. The smell of Russian tobacco hung heavily on the air and I could see along a small corridor into the bowels of the building.

A pleasant young Russian called Mikhail came out and spoke to me. I explained who I was. He told me that if I returned at 2 p.m., I could see Mr Prosvirin.

Further up the hill, I came to the Bishop's office. He was out but I spoke to him by phone at his home. He was sympathetic towards my idea of having public prayers for Irina in front of the Hallgrimmskirkja, telling me it was public land and a free country. I deposited my letters from church leaders and left for the Saga Hotel and the Hagaskoli.

The school playground had become the blustery parking lot for a couple of enormous satellite earth stations for BBC TV and a consortium of American companies respectively, flown in by Jumbo for the occasion.

The modern gym was fitted up with a video projector to cover the event, so the press men could see the pooled TV reporting of events such as the leaders arriving at Keflavik and entering and leaving the conference hall. There were marvellous displays about Icelandic wool and fishing products and a freezer full of free cartons of fruit juice from which you could take as many as you liked! To avail myself of all this, I needed a 'press card'.

144

The main concourse of the high school was a scrum of experienced press people who showed their press cards and were given a special one to dangle round their necks which admitted them to the press conferences of the summit. I opened my wallet and removed my precious letter from the *Church Times*. It seemed unlikely they'd accept this. The Icelanders took away my passport and letter, returned to question me about a few details and then presented me with my own red card to dangle round my neck. I was now an official reporter and mixed with the professionals. Brian Hanrahan was there, who reported the Falklands War, Christopher Walker, the Moscow correspondent of *The Times*, Peter Ruff of BBC Radio News, Martin Walker of *The Guardian*, and Martin Bell for BBC TV News, as well as reporters from the United States, Japan, Norway and France, to name but a few.

The timetable of events was pinned up on the board next to the telex which was churning out reports from the Press Association. President Reagan was arriving later that day and staying at the American Embassy. All houses within line of sight had been evacuated. Helicopters hovered overhead much of the time. Gorbachev would come tomorrow and stay on one of the two Soviet ships in the harbour. The Americans had hired a Norwegian cruise liner for their team. Raisa Gorbachev was going to visit a farm to see Icelandic sheep-rearing, and flights over the volcanic Westman Islands could be arranged for journalists wanting background stories about Iceland. The Icelanders had certainly prepared for the summit excellently considering they had only had a week's notice. It was an opportunity to put Iceland on the map for investors and the tourist industry, and they made a great success of it.

At 2 p.m. Mr Prosvirin came down to the crowded, bustling, bullet-proof lobby. He heard my story and accepted a letter from me, Paddy's card to Gorbachev, my letters of introduction and a gift-wrapped book of Irina's poetry. It was all very civil. Considering that the pace of life at a Soviet Embassy in this quiet North Atlantic port had suddenly quickened dramatically, I felt they received me very well.

My American contact hadn't arrived by the time I

called at their embassy and I was asked if I could come back tomorrow.

I wanted to check out with the Chief of Police my arrangements for a vigil for Irina in front of the Hall-grimmskirkja. I breezed into the police headquarters and asked if I could speak to Bodvar Bragasson, not Mr Bragasson, remembering what Agnethe had said. He was out, but his deputy was glad to see me. Karl Johansson greeted me like a long-lost friend and got me a cup of coffee as we had a chat. The Icelandic crime rate would be the envy of any other force in the world. Their police are un-armed and conduct themselves in a very civil fashion. Much of their work is on traffic duties. He was interested in the business about Irina and foresaw no difficulties, nor did the Mayor's deputy, David Oddsson. Both spoke up on behalf of their bosses without the fear that they might be stepping out of line, which was really impressive.

That evening there was to be a press conference given by the Soviet delegation at the Saga Hotel. I got there early, dangling my press card to secure my entry. A couple of hundred news reporters gathered in the large first-floor restaurant. I took a prominent table in the front row, pulled out my notepad and composed my question, writing in block capitals so I wouldn't have to fumble—I realized that I'd get no second chance.

The room filled up. The five-man delegation entered, led, so the interpreter told us, by Mr Albert Vlasov, First Deputy Head of the Propaganda Department of the Central Committee of the Communist Party. He gave an incon-sequential speech in Russian which was interpreted for us, after which questions were invited from the floor. I took the opportunity immediately, springing to my feet rather hastily. 'Rodgers, Church Times, London. Is it likely that Secretary Gorbachev will consider the release of the critically ill Soviet Christian poetess Irina Ratushinskaya, as a gesture of goodwill at the time of the summit conference, considering the concern expressed for her by the governments of Britain, France, Holland, Norway, Sweden and by the United States Congress and media?' I sat down. Vlasov turned to his colleagues and chuckled. My colleagues in the press corps showed they thought it was a good question, but one likely to cause a bit of embarrassment. The question got translated into Russian and was discussed. The answer came back. 'We do not think this will be on the agenda of the summit conference. Next question please!'

10

RELEASE

I didn't sleep well, and lay awake the next morning wondering whether I'd manage to stick it for forty-eight blustery hours outdoors in the world's most northern capital. I planned to put on my full clerical robes, cassock, surplice, academic hood and preaching scarf, and stand in front of a banner of Irina on the forecourt of the Hallgrimmskirkja. I'd start that Friday evening and try to last until Sunday evening, when I had to go to Keflavik for the plane the following morning. I didn't fancy my prospects, even though I'd brought my Russian hat and snow boots. The light was glimmering in the bit of cloudy sky which I could make out through the lace curtains.

The internal phone buzzed above my bed. I started and picked it up, but it didn't work. It was probably a call from England. There was no time to lose. I flung the door open and plummeted down the winding stairs into the little lobby. Motherly Inma handed me the receiver confirming that it was from England. It was Sue.

'Hello, love! Michael Bourdeaux of Keston wants you to ring him. Irina has been released from prison—unconditionally!'

I could hardly speak.

'When did it happen, love?'

'I think it was this morning!' Sue said.

'Oh that's great! That's great! Okay, love, I'll get in touch with Michael,' I exclaimed, still overcome with a mixture of disbelief and excitement.

She gave me the number, and I rang Michael Bourdeaux. He was overjoyed. It's the kind of news they long to hear in their kind of job, when so much of their time focuses on alerting people to the plight of prisoners in

148

communist countries. Irina had been told to get ready shortly before they let her go. The officials showed her a document from the Praesidium of the Supreme Soviet ordering her release. Then in the late afternoon, just before I asked my question at the press conference, they took her from her cell. She signed no plea, no declaration, nothing. They brought her out into the central courtyard of the Vladimirskaya Street Prison and told her to get into a black Volga car which was waiting for her.

The gates opened, then closed behind her as the car moved out into the street. They drove her some miles to the address in Vernadsky Avenue where Igor lived with his mother. The car waited with Irina still aboard while a prison official climbed the stairs to the flat to make sure someone was at home. Igor's mother answered the door. They told Irina to get out of the car and away they went.

Igor was still at work at the factory. His mother telephoned him and broke the news. He turned white and nearly fainted. His comrades wouldn't let him go, he looked so sick. However, he soon regained his composure and was home in a trice.

It was late and the phone was busy with friends calling excitedly. The grapevine had been activated! It's quite difficult getting a call to England and they didn't manage it that night. Alyona Kojevnikov, the information officer at Keston College, had been calling frequently to keep in touch and to encourage Igor, so they returned the call as soon as they could to share the glad news with her. Within a few minutes, Michael Bordeaux had informed the BBC. They interrupted the 8 a.m. Radio 4 news with a newsflash.

'It has just become known that Irina Ratushinskaya, the poetess who was in prison in the Soviet Union, has been freed and is at home with her husband in Kiev!'

Irina says, 'It was nice of them to take me home in the car. They could have just turned me out on the street and left me to get home on my own. Also, they didn't have to go up to check that there was someone at home. They could have just dumped me. It was nice of them!'

I wondered how long it takes to prepare an 'order of the Praesidium of the Supreme Soviet', and whether or not it had been decided to release Irina on that day! Does it have to be decided in a plenary session or is this the sort of order which would be issued by one or two officers of the Praesidium, rather like a little sub-committee? I should have loved to know. Perhaps I'll meet a friendly member of the Praesidium one day who'll be able to tell me. It's quite impressive to think that the Praesidium had to apply its 'mind' to Irina's case. Though maybe it was just a non-specific order which could be invoked to apply to any prisoner in particular circumstances.

Back in Iceland, I put the receiver down. I could still hardly believe it. I leant over the reception desk and gave Inma a tight hug, much to her surprise! I'd told her about Irina, but I think she was a bit taken aback at the idea of Mr Gorbachev acceding to the request of this rather eccentric hostel guest who lived on bully beef and rolls, when she had perfectly good Icelandic soused herring to offer! I wobbled up the stairs unsure of my footing, still in my pyjamas, and fell trembling on to my bed, sobbing a 'thank you' to God. I pulled on a few clothes, got out a bit of my headed note-paper, wrote a brief thank you note to Mr Gorbachev in block capitals and ran round to the Soviet Embassy. To their credit they opened the door to me even though it was still eight o'clock in the morning. I told them the news. Mikhail, the man on the door, accepted the letter and seemed pleased.

That morning I celebrated with soused herring at Inma's smorgasbord, and reflected on yesterday's press conference. Vlasov was right. Irina would not be on the agenda of the summit. I wondered whether he had known when he took my question. It turned out, in fact, that her release took place some three hours before I asked it! I got a bit muddled about the timing at first and had originally thought that she had been released on the same morning that I'd heard the news. As I munched my rolls and herring, an Ilyushin took off from a Soviet airfield with Mr Gorbachev on board, heading our way. Was Irina's release anything to do with my visit? Had I wasted my time? Perhaps it would have happened anyway! Probably it would, and yet, from a short list of some six or eight dissidents due to be released along with an American journalist named Daniloff, Irina was the only one to be chosen as a goodwill gesture at the time of the summit. There were no other Christian demonstrators there at Reykjavik as far as I could see. Something brought Irina's name forward to the front of the list and made her the prisoner of choice. How the choice was made, I just don't know.

Gudni Gunnarsson was at the door. We'd arranged to meet to plan Irina's vigil. He sat at the table as I finished the herrings. 'So she's out! That's wonderful! Are you going on with the vigil?'

'Yes, I think so,' I said. 'There's a chap who's very badly off called Alexander Ogorodnikov. He feels quite forgotten in prison and is begging to be shot. I must do it for him.'

Gudni complied, bless him. He would come up and we would go over the site together. He promised to bring some students along in the evening. I still had to get the news of Irina's release around. I knew that Steingrimmur Hermannsson, the Prime Minister of Iceland, was going to give a live TV press conference at the Television Centre near the conference centre. Gudni drove me along and left me to it. The Prime Minister was about to go into the press conference. One of the Icelanders at the press centre had kindly delivered a book of Irina's poetry to him for me the night before. Few press reporters attended, but the coverage was live, so after a few questions, I made up my rather devious pseudo-question—just to get on the air. I complimented the Prime Minister on the friendly spirit which the choice of a meeting in Iceland had already given to the talks and asked him whether he would like to comment on the release of Irina Ratushinskaya as at least one tangible result of the summit so far. He and the chairman realized that this wasn't really a question, but they took it in good spirits and he said that he was delighted with the news. I knew a delegation of American Jews was holding a press conference about the thousands of refuseniks who were being kept from emigrating to join their families in Israel and the West. I thought Arieh Handler would be there, the leading British Jew who supported me so well and came to the cage at St

Martin's. I retraced my steps along the old streets and up on to the bluff across the open ground towards the Hagaskoli. I was still on a 'high', not heeding the blustery showers and muttered my thankfulness to God as I scampered along, full of the joys of spring, even on this cold October day.

I passed a booth on the edge of an open field of volcanic ash, where a man was selling flowers. I had an idea and stopped to buy a small bunch of rather pricey carnations. The Jews had already started. The press were there in force. Relatives of Ida Nudel were there. Mothers stood up who had been awaiting the arrival of their children from the Soviet Union for ten years. It was a sombre occasion. I recognized some British Jewish faces on the panel. I couldn't see Arieh Handler though I knew he was in Iceland. At the end of the speeches I stepped forward and presented the chairman with the bunch of carnations as a tribute to the help given by British Jews in working for the release of Irina Ratushinskaya. 'She was released this morning and is at home with her husband in Kiev.' (This was before I realized that her release had been the previous day.)

They were delighted. It was kind of them to take it that way; they could have turfed me out of their press conference if they'd felt so inclined. It got the news on German television and my architect cousin in Stuttgart rang my Mum and Dad to say that he and his German wife had been watching the evening news and had seen me present the flowers and make my speech. It also got on several of the American networks, and I then did an interview with John Silverman for *The World at One*, as well as with Dutch Radio and Voice of America. The *Sunday* programme and *Woman's Hour* also gave it high priority.

I didn't know what to do after that. The American diplomat who had agreed to see me was in a meeting, so I went to the State Opening of the Icelandic Parliament. The members of the *Althing* processed past me into the dolls-house cathedral on the main square, not to be confused with the Hallgrimmskirkja on the crest of the hill. It was like something out of Alice in Wonderland. The elegant Vigdis Finnbogadottir sat with poise on an armchair throne in front of the cathedral's box pews. The big Lutheran priest led the prayers facing away from the congregation towards the altar and then disappeared round a corner, to emerge with a struggle through a tiny door in the wall at the back of an equally tiny pulpit. I don't know whether he was over-awed by the presence of the mighty, or whether the geothermal central heating was turned up too high, but the sweat trickled off his forehead, which he mopped with a sodden handkerchief between every couple of sentences.

After the service, I was met by Mark Parris, the head of the Soviet Bureau of the American State Department. I had to check in at the United States Embassy first, which was quite a job, but at last Mr Parris came and ushered me up the narrow winding stair to the second floor. We sat at a desk in a disused classroom overlooking the old town. We congratulated each other. He admitted he was responsible for working on a lot of the cases of dissidents and was personally very relieved about the good news of Irina. I liked him. He was straightforward, thirty-five to forty, slim and shirt-sleeved. He told me a fair bit about the Daniloff exchange, and accepted the book of poetry, the letters of recommendation and the card from Paddy, promising to give them to the President. We chatted for quite a while and I told him about Ogorodnikov, to discover that he already knew the story in great detail. We parted and he said he was sure that the President would be particularly touched by Paddy's card.

A month later Paddy received a letter on White House notepaper, saying what a brave lad he was and how much Paddy's prayers had contributed to Irina's release, signed Ronald Reagan. The President wrote to me also apologizing that he'd not been able to see me in Iceland. He said he had kept in his drawer in the Oval office an appeal which had been sent to him by some women in the same camp as Irina. On receiving my letter, he went over to the drawer and pulled out the appeal. Irina's name was among the signatures on it. He had read the book of poetry and found it very moving. He said that it meant a lot to him to have it. I was impressed. It wasn't a word-processor letter. I had heard about the appeal from other sources as well.

Wood is scarce in Iceland. I scoured Reyjkavik for

some timber on to which to secure my banner of Irina for the vigil, and at dusk I dragged all the bits and pieces up to the church, starting the vigil in front of the banner. The light faded. Gudni's wife brought a big candle, but it wouldn't light in the wind. Driving rain started to thrash down, my clerical robes became sodden. The dye ran, staining my surplice with the mauve of my academic hood. Snow boots, I discovered, are snow boots. They aren't made for rain and mine quickly soaked it up leaving my feet standing in puddles inside the plastic soles.

A man walked by with his dog. 'What's it all about?' he enquired in English, once he discovered my lack of Icelandic. I was staying out here for forty-eight hours, I explained, to publicize the plight of a man in prison in Russia. It looks like a woman in your picture, not a man. The banner fluttered behind me on the posts propped against a low wall and lashed to a park bench. 'Yes,' I explained, 'that was Irina. They let *her* out this morning.' It might have sounded rather impressive but somehow it didn't come over like that. 'Oh yes,' he said. The dog got fidgety, so the man walked on, wishing me luck.

The wind howled. I heard a crash. The banner had blown forward like a Viking sail and crashed down on the paving stones behind me, bringing the park bench with it. I got tangled up in the dark and wet, not knowing which bits were part of my surplice and which bits were banner. They were both equally soggy and mud-stained. The banner ripped along one edge of the wooden beam leaving the drawing pins and a ribbon of cotton pathetically attached. I struggled to patch it up and reef it in.

A car stopped and a young mother got out after struggling with the child safety seat in the back. She came over. In the dark, illuminated by the street lamps, she was very graceful, her fair hair flowing like a Viking's, and her slim figure clutching her child to her hip.

'What are you doing?' she enquired. She didn't bother with Icelandic; I obviously wasn't one of them.

I told her about Irina, about Alexander, and his sewage-flooded cell, about the fact that he had only had a single visit by his wife in eight years, about his plea to be shot. It was raining but those weren't raindrops on her cheeks. She wept for Alexander, Igor, Irina.

'It's terrible,' she said, 'I'm so sorry. It's so easy for us here in Iceland, we can do whatever we like.'

The words penetrated straight to my heart. Showing me the child in her arms, staring up at us from a tiny anorak, she told me, 'His name means "trust" in Icelandic.'

She wished me well, reinstated 'Trust' into his child seat and with a last good wish she was gone.

Her visit persuaded me to stick it out. But the rain was lashing down between occasional clearer patches when the wind dried the outer layer of my robes a little. It might even have been better if it had been a few degrees colder, at least the snow would have blown off my clothes instead of saturating them.

It all seemed ill-conceived. I'd press-released it but nobody came. Of course, this wasn't the story they had been sent to get. They couldn't risk coming to see me in case they missed some of the main action. It would have been hard to explain back in London or Washington or Tokyo.

As I stood with my back to the church, with the statue of Leifur Eriksson, the Viking discoverer of Vinland (America) looming down behind me, I faced down one of the city's main shopping streets. I stood at a junction, watching cars pass. The drivers peered out through the darkness and the rain to see this strange apparition in the light of the street lamps. The Icelanders are a delightful people but they are a bit relaxed about their driving. Just then a car overshot the junction and took out a street lamp just next to me. The street was now a little darker and I had a legitimate, face-saving excuse for packing up and going home before I witnessed any more accidents or froze to death. I was relieved that the police didn't seem to bother about me.

Demoralized and disgusted with myself I packed up shop and trudged home to my cosy room at the Salvation Army hostel. I had taken the precaution of not booking myself out!

Gudni turned up with his students a few minutes after

I'd left and I've never really made it up to him. He must have felt a bit stood up.

The hostel felt like heaven after that lot. My face glowed. I had a volcanic shower to recuperate, and a sound sleep before getting back out there the next morning. There were more dry spells but the rain didn't go away.

Reagan and Gorbachev met, and I followed their progress by seeing where the helicopters were buzzing around. There wasn't really much news for the reporters but even the little there was evidently did not include me. It was very frustrating shivering in the cold wind, seeing all the action at a distance and not being part of it. Gudni came back and explained that they had come last night. I apologized. A few more showers, and at midday I called the whole thing off. I didn't fancy another evening out on the town.

I stacked my bits and pieces in my room and couldn't think what to do next except fly back to London. I sat in the warm and stared at the wall for an hour, my face aglow from the north-atlantic weather. This wouldn't do. I dragged myself up to the press centre again. I was glad of that press card. My press release about the vigil had been torn from the notice board at the press centre, so no wonder no one knew anything about it. After three cups of coffee and a few half-hearted attempts to talk to media people, I rang Sue and posted a lot of postcards to European campaigning colleagues. The final press conference of the summit left everyone feeling very despondent. Yet I, for all the disappointment about the aborted vigil, rejoiced quietly over the good news from Kiev.

I spent a pleasant evening at the Bjarnarssons's house near the NATO base discussing Iceland and the long nights, then early in the morning Hermann ran me to the airport. Sue, Christopher and Timothy were all at Heathrow to meet me. We had a lovely reunion, then went straight back to Birmingham where Michael Bourdeaux was booked to address a big crowd in a city-centre church that evening. There was great thankfulness as they heard my story. Apparently, the proceedings at Keston College Open Day the previous Saturday had been interrupted by Alyona coming in to report that she'd just been on the phone to Kiev and had spoken to Irina at her home!

Irina had had a lot to say! She repeatedly spoke of her deep gratitude to all her readers, and to all those who had campaigned for her release over the past three years. She was convinced that it was this support that was the key factor in her release. In the camp they knew that people in the West were praying for them.

'All of us in the women's political zone felt this support and prayer in a way that is impossible to describe in mere words.' (That's really saying something for a poet of Irina's calibre!) 'It is practically a physical sensation, a sort of screen which protects you from everything that is being done to you,' Irina explained.

She'd certainly continue to write poetry. 'This is my form of communication, it is my life. I cannot live without it. It would be a special joy if my poems were published in my own country. When I write, I address myself, in the first instance, to my own people.'

As for plans, she very much wanted to come for treatment in the West and to visit her supporters and readers. She dictated a special message:

'My mother was the first to give me life. But that life, and the possibility to go on working, was returned to me by a vast number of people from all over the world. Now, as never before, I feel my kinship with all people. I rejoice in this, and will strive to justify the confidence that has been demonstrated in me by all of you.'

It appears that soon after Irina's release, the 'small zone' was shut down and the prisoners dispersed to prisons nearer their homes. Almost all have subsequently been released.

After a week or two of rejoicing, it soon became evident that we couldn't leave Irina and go on to work for someone else. The KGB were harassing her and Igor and quizzing their friends. Often the operator would say that there was nobody at home when in fact it turned out that there was. Letters still went astray a great deal and when the postman said there was a parcel to collect, Igor would go for it only to discover that it had been collected on their behalf by someone else supposedly 'authorized' to collect it, presumably the KGB. Radio jamming seemed to be particularly bad around their flat. One agonizing snatch from a Western broadcast, which Irina managed to catch, reported that she didn't want to leave the Soviet Union. On the contrary, Irina managed to let it be known that it was her first priority to take up an invitation to come to Britain for medical treatment. It was thought quite feasible that Western journalists ringing their phone number were actually being diverted to talk to another woman with a similar voice who was a KGB operative.

Irina's health, although improving, was still bad but she vowed she would not accept medical treatment from any Soviet doctor since they all have a recognized prior responsibility to the state which overrides any responsibility to individual patients.

Back in May, we had started moves to get Igor and Irina a formal invitation to visit Britain. The *Church Times* published my request for pledges of money to cover the costs of her medical and other expenses so that I could realistically tell the Home Office that she needn't be a drain on public funds.

Tim Renton wrote to me saying they would try to transmit the invitation, but since Irina was then in a labour camp, it was most unlikely to come to anything. I had to fill in a form called a Statutory Declaration, one for Igor and one for Irina, to promise first, that they wanted to come to Britain on a visit and second, that I could support them. People wrote in with £9,000 worth of pledges of financial support in the event of her being able to come. Each declaration had to be signed in front of a solicitor at a small charge of £3.

Her address changed when she was moved to Kiev, so new forms had to be made out and my declaration authenticated again. Then Irina arrived home; another change of address, more forms. The Passport and Immigration Office ran out of forms.

When I had got it right as far as I could, the Foreign Office sent the forms off to Moscow to the British Embassy, who got in touch with Igor. I had his date of birth wrong and the Russian Visa Office had rejected it. So I corrected the date of birth and went through the whole rigmarole again. This time the Visa Office in Kiev pointed out the wrong middle name for Irina. It was not acceptable. Another trip to London, another visit to the solicitor, another fee, and another visit to Immigration. I had to make about six attempts to get it right.

Igor and Irina came up by train to Moscow, to collect a document from the British Embassy promising them that they'd be given a British entry visa if the Soviets would let them come. Igor's works wouldn't release him, so he resigned to enable them to make this journey. Without a job, he would be liable to imprisonment within four months. It's hard for Soviet citizens to get into Western Embassies. Soviet guards outside the gate are under orders to prevent entry. Seven Pentecostals got stranded for years in the American Embassy after making a dash past the Soviet guards and risking getting shot. To avoid this pitfall, a member of the Embassy staff kindly waited on the embankment of the Moscow River outside the Embassy to rendezvous with Igor and Irina and escort them safely past their Soviet 'protectors'. On their return they took my invitation to the Visa Office.

'No,' the official said a few days later. 'The details are all correct now, but the application for a visa has been rejected because an invitation by a friend in a capitalist country is not a good enough reason for leaving the Soviet Union.'

They didn't, of course, tell us that in the first place. I think they had been hoping to shake us off by their rejections of the paperwork. Now they'd run out of excuses, it was just a plain 'Niet'.

I couldn't let my efforts drop now that Igor had jeopardized his freedom specifically to receive my personal invitation. Others had issued invitations, but I think that mine was the only one to get past all the hurdles of paperwork as far as the stage of a flat rejection. The Russians, Americans and British met together again in Vienna at a review conference to check on whether each was keeping the terms of the Helsinki Agreement on Human Rights. It was the ideal place to go to represent Irina's plight and press for a solution. Unfortunately, I missed it through not reading the newspaper and only learned of the date of the conference the day before it happened. But others went and her case was mentioned.

I wrote to the Archbishop of Canterbury who kindly saw me for a long meeting in his Church House office, during a meeting of the General Synod. He was already very concerned about Irina and helped a lot. I tried to get a motion put to Synod to press for a resolution on Irina's plight, but the agenda was already overfull. We prayed for her in chapel instead and the Bishop of Worcester spoke up for her.

People asked me if I'd ever spoken to Irina on the phone. After all, she and Igor were in regular contact with someone in England, albeit a Russian speaker, Alyona. Nicholas Kojevnikov rang her from the BBC Russian Service and recorded an uninterrupted forty-five-minute conversation with her.

'This is how it ought to be,' he rejoiced. No unseen listener had pulled the plug on them—an almost unheard of liberty of communication. I got hold of the number and arranged the call with the operator. A few minutes later, the phone rang and after a few clicks and bumps a male voice answered in Russian.

'Ah, Igor. Is that you? This is Dick in England.'

'Ah, I'm pleased to hear you, Dick.'

He went and got Irina and we had a short but delightful conversation the gist of which was, 'I am very happy to hear you, Dick!' It was mutual, to put it mildly! Over the phone to Alyona she dictated numerous poems, including one dedicated to me. Alyona translated it for me:

DO NOT BREAK UP THAT CAGE
Somewhere far, far away
Is a land I have known of from childhood
Out of books,
Fraying maps.
White cliffs rise from the sea
As from far-away dreams.
How I dread to awaken
And find myself back in the camps.

Somewhere, there, they awaited me
Even as I thought to die.
There my friend shared my cell and privations
In an iron-barred cage.
Over there, starved of news
They were deaf to all lies
And discounting the years sought
to save me from dying.
I would write, but the mail goes astray
And the phone has been silenced
Since yesterday morning.
I would fly
But invisible bonds chain my shoulders.
Do not break up that cage, my dear friend,
For the time is not yet—
Let it be, though
The last in Creation!
Irina Ratushinskaya
Kiev, 30 October 1986

It was a mixture of a terrific compliment and my marching orders. I must not stop. I had got a bit muddled up about her and Alexander Ogorodnikov. Having said on the radio that I was starting to work for Alexander's release, I did just that. But, in consequence, had less time and energy left to work for Irina. It was a great relief when a New Zealander called Athanasius, otherwise known as 'Chris', told me he was proposing to fast totally for Advent out of solidarity for Alexander. 'Athanasius' was a religious name he had taken when he became an 'Orthodox' Christian. He carves icons in wood and wants to be a monk. We got him a church in which to base his vigil, in the centre of London. And away he went!

I was free again to turn my attention to Irina. I thought things were brewing under the surface and that the Soviets might be biding their time, waiting for something, but it was really important not to seem to forget about her. For months, I'd wanted to get over to the Continent to meet those who were concerned with people in Russia in a similar way to myself. I was about to print a whole lot of appeal postcards for the Continentals to send to their respective

Soviet Ambassadors, to plead for Irina and Igor's visas. Instead, I went with about 40 kilos of postcards pleading for Alexander's release, 2,000 for each country, in their own language. We covered France, Germany and Holland, with bilingual editions for Switzerland and Belgium. Others for Norway, Sweden and Australia were distributed by travellers. The load in my suitcase nearly pulled my arm off!

Just before I left for Paris on 10 December, word came through that the Visa Office had contacted Igor and Irina and had asked them to come in a few days for an appointment. I hesitated, but nothing was certain yet, so I decided to go and make as much use of my tour as I could for stirring things up internationally, both for Irina and for Alexander. At Dover, I met a man who asked me where I was going with my heavy suitcase. I explained.

'You don't think you'll get her out, do you?'

'Yes. She'll be coming soon!'

In Paris, the phone rang in the flat where I was staying. It was my Birmingham agent on the line. 'Hello, love! Igor and Irina have been told to go and collect visas tomorrow.' It was all getting rather real!

The next evening, after linking up with two excellent and vigorous French campaigning groups, I looked round for a coin box which would take international calls. I slid my *telecarte* into the slot and dialled. Sue's voice. 'They've got their visa. They hope to come late next week.'

On to Brussels, where my hosts let me ring Sue. 'Igor and Irina have got all their travel documents and they're hoping to get a British Airways flight on Thursday or Friday.' It was Monday evening. I had to cut out Zurich and Berlin! But I worked out that if I hurried I could fit in Antwerp. A quick call to Sue from Mrs Van Cutsem's flat in that city: 'Yes, love, they've left Kiev on the overnight train to Moscow. They're going to stay with friends in the city and they're booked on flight BA711 arriving Heathrow at 18.55 on Thursday.'

I hurried back to London and rang home from my parents' home. Yes, I was glad. Sue wanted to come down to the airport. What about Christopher? Should she take him out of school? 'Yes, please. I don't want him to miss this for anything!' After breakfast and a bit more phoning around I set off into town. I linked up with the reception party and scurried round London so busy telling the press that I forgot I had an invitation to do a bit for the BBC Nine O'clock News in the studios at Shepherd's Bush—that's pretty busy! I wouldn't normally miss that!

I got hold of the PR office at Heathrow and liaised with Air Traffic Control through them. At 17.15 I rang them again. Air Traffic Control at West Drayton confirmed that the aircraft had taken off from Moscow. They had cleared Soviet airspace bound for London and were out over the Baltic flying at 35,000 feet.

11

WE MEET AT LAST

At Heathrow, I made my way to Terminal One.

We waited at Arrivals, by the gate that Irina and Igor would come through. A permanent crowd-control barrier kept waiting relatives and friends away from the automatic frosted-glass doors in the frosted-glass wall. The doors would open from time to time to reveal someone trundling a trolley with a suitcase and bag of duty-frees. I tracked down the Hon. David Astor, the Chairman of the Irina Trust, who was going to look after arrangements with the press and try to keep them under control. I had a look at the press room which we had been offered for a press conference in the Queen's Building next door.

Two pairs of footsteps resounded outside, along with the squeaking wheels of a baby buggy. Sue and Christopher appeared round the door with Tiny Tim's face peering out of the wraps on the buggy. Other members of my family also arrived. Back in 'Arrivals' a crowd had gathered expectantly. David Astor's assistant told me she'd heard from the British Embassy in Moscow. A member of the Embassy staff had escorted Igor and Irina out to the airport and seen them safely through Soviet Customs and Visa control. They were definitely on the plane. It was a bit delayed and still out over the North Sea, but was due to land in an hour.

The crowd built up, and the TV crews and press men gathered round. 'British Airways announce the arrival of flight BA711 from Moscow.' I carried Christopher in my arms. Sue carried Timothy. We pressed forward to the rail. Each time the door opened we peered into the distance.

There she is. 'Irina! Irina! Irina!' A little dark-haired head, the one from the banners and posters, glided along escorted by two tall men, still inside the customs hall. I recognized David Astor on one side, and then Igor, who held her firmly by the arm. David supported her on the other side, her small wan face expectantly looking out from beneath her simple, straight-cropped dark hair.

She walked through the sliding door and out into the main concourse. People clapped and cheered, shouting 'Irina! Irina!' She smiled timidly. I climbed over the barrier and stepped forward still holding Christopher in my arms.

'Hello, Irina! I'm Dick. It's lovely that you have arrived!' I said, presenting her with a bunch of flowers.

'Oh, Deek! I am very pleased to meet you.' She smiled and kissed me, this woman, who until now had been locked in a prison camp thousands of miles away. It was wonderful to see her—a visible answer to so many people's prayers.

I don't remember many words. We all came to a standstill. I probably said something inane like 'I'm very pleased to meet you too!' after which I greeted Igor.

There was a lot of jostling. Flash bulbs cascaded, TV crews pushed forward and the crowd heaved like a wave in a sea cavern. Irina's frail figure in the middle seemed in danger of being crushed. David Astor ordered the press to clear the way. The pair of them, gripping her firmly and protectively by the arm, motored her through the crowd at a snail's pace, festooned with flowers. A punch-up followed. The TV cameramen were walking backwards in front of her. Others could not get near, so sprinted on ahead to over-take the crowd. They clambered up the concrete stanchions holding up the roof. Zacchaeus would have been proud of their performance! Another fellow with a camera who stood his ground in front of them, got summary treatment from his colleagues. They grabbed him by the collar and flung him to one side. When she was later asked how she coped with it, Irina commented, 'They're gentler than the Ukrainian KGB!' David and Igor kept going, and Irina survived. They walked in through the door of the Queen's Building and into the conference room, where they were glad to sit down for a breather. The crowd thinned, and the bouncers kept out the rest of the crowd. I felt for Irina's beloved supporters, some of whom had come hundreds of miles to see her. David Astor explained that Irina and Igor were too tired to answer questions but that they did have a statement to make.

'I am very grateful to all people of good wish who have worked to bring about my freedom,' said Irina. 'I am glad that the first soil on which I have been really free is this British soil.' She expressed her concern for those left behind in the camp and in other camps. She sat there, poised, enunciating her words with poetic clarity, taking great pains to form the English words correctly, drawing out her lips and forming her mouth as if to puff out a candle. Igor then made a statement which was translated into English. Christopher and I squatted in the corner amongst all the cables, though we had lost sight of Sue by this time.

The entourage stood waiting for some shots of the pair of them, who were holding a big bunch of flowers. Then, on the two male arms, she edged her way out of the press room and along the corridor, followed by the scrum of supporters and reporters who still wanted to see her. Irina was thin, particularly when one realized that she had already put on three stone in the last few months. It turned out that on New Year's Day, 1986 she was so emaciated that she could easily feel her spine through her tummy.

There were excellent pictures of Irina on the national news, followed by plenty more over the next few days.

The following morning, she and Igor went to the hospital. Irina appeared to the doctors to be in the early stages of recovery from severe malnutrition. She was very frail and priorities for necessary treatment were determined.

We slept in on Friday. In the afternoon I went over to Alyona's house, where Irina and Igor were staying, and found David Sells of *Newsnight* and his crew interviewing them. Once more, I crouched on the floor and took in the scene. It was hard to believe that it was all real. News had come of the Sakharovs being allowed to return from exile in Gorky and while I was there the phone went with a report of Dzhemilyov, a Crimean Tartar human-rights activist, having been released from prison. Igor and Irina danced for joy in the kitchen. It was small enough but you could hardly see where you were going for the bunches of flowers everywhere! Igor gave me a gift of a pair of prettily embroidered linen tablecloths which his mother had made especially for me. I shook his hand, looked him in the face and thanked him. He gave a big, broad toothy grin, muttered something positive in Russian and slapped me on the shoulder!

Over the weekend they were able to rest a little. On Sunday they worshipped at the Russian Church in Ennismore Gardens.

What a day Monday was! It started with a press conference at the Foreign Correspondents' Association in Carlton House Terrace. I gave out a medical bulletin and assumed my accustomed position, squatting on the floor at the front on the right. We all stressed that Irina was pretty frail and might have to stop answering questions if it got too much for her. She talked of her concern for those who were left behind. She said she was not going back to the Soviet Union, until she would be safe from arrest. She thought things would have to change a lot in the Soviet Union for that to be the case. Irina was reserved when asked about *Glasnost*, the new Soviet policy of openness, saying that it should be weighed by its results not its promises. She gave some staggering figures about the number of people still in camps for political or religious reasons. Someone asked, 'How did you write your poems in the camp?' 'I wrote my rhymes (she kept calling them her 'rhymes') on bars of soap with a matchstick or any pointed object I could find. It was a good way of doing it. If I made a mistake I could rub it out. I would keep it there until I had memorized it, and then when I was sure I had done so, I would wash my hands with the soap and it would be gone.'

Asked how she got the poems out, she would not say, but she had memorized 240 poems in camp and composed about three a week for a lot of the time. I could see what her fellow prisoners meant when they called her a person of lively and precise mind.

The next question came from the correspondent of the *Church Times*. 'How did you start writing poetry? Did you write when you were a child?'

This gave Irina the chance to talk a little about her childhood. 'When I was five, I told my mother I would like to travel to Africa and see monkeys and crocodiles. My mother said, "Oh no! You wouldn't be allowed!" "Why?" I asked, "who wouldn't allow me? The crocodiles?" "No," my mother replied, "not the crocodiles, our government wouldn't allow you." From that moment, I decided I would rather deal with crocodiles.'

The whole place fell apart laughing, even the serious news reporters who had been sent to get a comment about *Glasnost* or arms control! It seemed the time to move. She rose to her feet and her strong-arm men glided her out, down the impressive stairs and into the waiting car.

I went on foot to Downing Street. Once the car arrived, we all presented ourselves at the door of Number Ten. I walked up the street behind the car as the rest entered the Prime Minister's Residence. The smartly dressed men inside didn't turn me away. They took our coats, and we mounted the stairs. The group of pool photographers clicked away as Mrs Thatcher greeted Igor and Irina in front of the Christmas tree. We went for coffee in the drawing room, a beautiful airy room with big windows overlooking Horseguards Parade and St James's Park.

Mrs Thatcher had read Irina's poetry and complimented her on it. She was very concerned about the whole scene from which Irina and Igor had emerged. Michael Bourdeaux was there too and Alyona sat behind the couple dovetailing her phrases between those of the Prime Minister. As we stood to go, Michael introduced me. The Prime Minister and her Parliamentary Private Secretary, Michael Allison, knew about the Irina Vigil and my time in the cage and we exchanged a few words before going downstairs.

Tim Renton received us on the other side of the street. We entered by the back door of the Foreign Office and went up to his waiting room. Irina was a bit weak by then. David Astor became protective, so the chat took place there in the Ambassadors' waiting room instead, of going further on to Mr Renton's office. It had to be brief and to the point. He was delighted to welcome them, and wished them well. This was the culmination of some hard work by Mr Renton and his staff. It must have been with some satisfaction that they watched the couple leave to make a new life together. Once back to the car, they motored over to Chelsea and relaxed for a few hours at David Astor's place. I celebrated with a steak and kidney pie at what used to be Lyons Corner House opposite Charing Cross Station and arrived at David Astor's house mid-afternoon, ready for a lift to Lambeth Palace. An independent television crew was there. I squatted on the floor. Each time we met, Igor and Irina greeted me warmly with a broad smile. Igor gave me a handshake and Irina, a slavic kiss on the cheek.

Arriving at Lambeth I got out of the car and pulled the same bell as I had done three months before on the way to Reykjavik. The Archbishop was finishing a carol service for the Palace staff. We waited a few minutes at the gate lodge.

When we entered by the main palace door and climbed the grand flight of stairs, the Archbishop was waiting at the top. He greeted us all, and ushered us along the long oak-panelled corridors, past the portraits of his predecessors and into the chapel. The rest of the party stayed back as he ushered Igor and Irina forward to the sanctuary. They stood calmly before him, their heads bowed. He prayed over them and blessed them in their new life together. It looked like a wedding. We kept silence and thanked God for delivering Irina from prison. The Archbishop didn't say much in public. But he's been a very good friend to Igor and Irina.

Then the shouting started and the harrowing business of passing from Soviet austerity to the bourgeois life of the market-place. The press wanted the story. They were insistent and abrupt, and sometimes over-stepped the limits of courtesy. I was glad to be out of it, although sometimes I felt for those who had helped a lot and couldn't get a look in, crowded out by their more vociferous competitors. It was a tricky business managing Irina's public relations and it's small wonder there was sometimes a bit of friction. Irina joked that the press imposed an extension of her sentence! She and Igor got away to the country for a few days over Christmas and wrote out some of the 240 poems which they had both memorized; doubling up to safeguard against slips of the memory.

As Sue and I watched television over Christmas, we saw Irina and Igor on the news visiting 'Athanasius' as he ended his fast for Alexander Ogorodnikov. Seven weeks later, Alexander was set free and returned to Moscow. The joy was muted, however, by the sadness which met him on his arrival. His wife had married another man five days before Alexander's release from prison. This prevented him from getting a residence permit, putting him, once more, under threat of arrest and unable to avail himself of the custody of his ten-year-old son to which his ex-wife had agreed. What a mess! Alexander has retained his poise in the jubilation and in the sadness.

On the first Sunday in January we were in London again. I brought Irina and Igor over to Mum and Dad's house on a dark and dismal afternoon, for tea. We took a stroll in the wintry twilight amongst the dripping hornbeam trees near the house. Then the couple sat on the sofa and Dad told them in a formal voice, 'It is a great joy and a great privilege to have you here, Irina. We thank God for your release.' He wanted to get the proper greeting in before we got on with the gossip. Irina commented that when they got up in the morning, they could hardly believe their eyes when they drew the curtain and saw London! They didn't eat much. Irina and Igor didn't appear to have voracious appetites. They played with Christopher and Timothy and we all enjoyed their company very much, although they were pretty exhausted from talking English all afternoon by the time I took them home.

Irina remained in great demand and travelled with Igor to Vienna to brief the Conference on Human Rights and to Rotterdam to receive a prize for her poetry. Lots of people wanted to send her gifts or to invite her to their church. It was a stressful time for them.

I spent an evening with her to glean more information for this book. It was a hard evening for her, although she kindly gave me quite a bit to go on. Irina is a tremendously precise and disciplined person. She would never have managed to memorize all her poems otherwise, and she reckons she has not forgotten a single one.

We met in the front room with a group who prayed

when Irina was in prison. We sang a hymn, prayed and asked Irina if she'd like to say something. She thanked them for their concern for her. 'My life depended on it.' She has expressed this to all the groups and individuals who have worked for her release, myself included.

Later on, we wanted to take Igor and Irina to Birmingham. It was February, and Sue and I and the boys had been invited to have lunch with Bishop Colin Buchanan and Di, his wife. Irina's health was still rather unpredictable; and she couldn't commit herself far in advance. The Buchanans kind-heartedly leapt at the opportunity to meet Irina and Igor and laid on a buffet for lots of other guests as well!

Distinguished guests agreed to read lessons, sing and generally take part in a service, which we advertised over the radio, TV and in the press. We suggested that people could bring flowers. St Martin's was the obvious place, but would it feel a bit empty? It held a thousand people and ten days wasn't long to get the news around, especially since we'd run out of money even for postage stamps!

I collected Irina and Igor from London. At Euston, we met up with Professor Geoffrey Hosking, a fluent Russian speaker who had kindly agreed to interpret. He had a genius for helping them relax. I'd mugged up a copy of the diary which the women smuggled out of the camp, and noticed some fascinating little give-away lines in it.

'It says in the diary of the camp that the woman whom you thought was a KGB informer threatened to murder you and your cat! Did you really have a cat in the "small zone"?' I asked.

'Yes we did! We called her Nyurka,' replied Irina. 'She was our friend. She was very good at catching rats and mice, and the barracks were infested with them. We used to feed her with our food. When we were about to go on hunger strike we'd keep a bit by for her on the few days leading up to the strike. One day, when I was on hunger-strike, Nyurka came and brought me presents of mice, because she thought I looked hungry. She brought them in her mouth and dropped them at my feet, expectantly. I had to explain to her that when you're on hunger-strike you're not even allowed to eat mice!

'She was really good to us. When we political prisoners were on hunger strike she'd still catch mice but she'd begun to eat them around the corner out of sight of any of us, so as not to torment us. She could get in and out of the "small zone" to get the mice and rats. She could get through the fences as easy as anything. She was really clever. We said she was a really "political cat". It was mostly the Lithuanian woman, Jadvyga Bieliavskiene, who knew about cats and looked after her when she had kittens. So the kittens all had Lithuanian names. The guards used to have rats and mice in their quarters too, so we gave them Nyurka's kittens as presents and now there are a lot of cats in the guards' quarters all with Lithuanian names!'

'You gave the guards presents!' I asked disbelievingly.

'Oh yes,' Irina replied. 'We got on quite well with the guards and many of them tried to help us. They hated Podust (the section leader) as much as we did. She was terrible to them almost as much as she was terrible to us. She dressed beautifully when we were in rags. She was a real sadist.'

'What's this about Podust being moved but waiting till her children finished the school year before going?' I enquired.

'Podust had a family, although the prisoners didn't know much about her husband. I don't imagine they got on very well,' Irina surmised. 'I think he had something to do with the prison service too. She's been moved to Tambov to look after a place where children are kept, poor things.'

'Also, it says that in the barrack room you had a television. Could you really watch television in labour camp?'

'Oh yes—it was only Soviet television, of course!—but yes, we had television and we sometimes watched it in the evening after work.'

'What time did you finish work?'

'It depended on how much work we had to do.'

'Didn't you have a set norm of gloves you had to make?'

'Well, yes, but in practice it varied a bit.'

Irina's routine started early. Her reveille was at 6 a.m. They started work in the sewing room at 8 a.m. and worked eight hours a day for six days a week. The noise of all the machines in a confined space became very stressful, and they weren't allowed to move from them during working hours. The foreman in charge of glove production was a good man by the name of Vasili Petrovich. He was aged around fifty or fifty-five years old, and quite fair to them. His responsibilities included other parts of the camp and he had to ensure that he made enough gloves in total. He would not overstretch the women and when they were on hunger strike, although they had to work, he let them get away with a lower rate of production. At other times he would ask for their help when the men in zone so-and-so were on strike and he'd fall behind his norm if they didn't make a bit more headway. So the women would always help. After all, if he was replaced, they might end up with someone a lot worse. The work was supposed to finish for a meal at 7 p.m. but in practice it varied with the workload as agreed with the foreman. Lights out was at 10 p.m.

A former prisoner, Avraham Shifrim, mentions some of the other things prisoners are expected to produce, including the rather delightful looking sets of wooden nesting dolls painted by 'folk artists' which any visitor to the Soviet Union will have seen. It makes sense really. They must be very laborious to make and any other sort of labour would make the price prohibitive. Prisoners also produce the beautiful lacquered, decorated wooden spoons and bowls which make very nice souvenirs. The little bear, "Mishka", the mascot of the 1980 Moscow Olympics, is a plastic injection moulding done, apparently, in the camps. Some Soviet sweets are produced by prisoners. Women prisoners on the Soviet islands north of Japan produce black caviare by gutting and processing the fish landed by the Soviet Far East fleet from the icy waters of the northern Pacific Ocean.

Any prisoner meeting the daily norm of seventy gloves gets a monthly payment of five roubles (just under £5) to spend in the camp shop. Anyone exceeding the norm gets seven roubles a month. That is roughly what I paid for one matrioshka doll. The workers obviously don't get fair return for their labour in spite of working in a socialist economy!

173

What was all this about Irina's head being shaved? It turns out that she did it herself—not that that makes much difference. She had sores all over her scalp, I imagine because of the bugs, fleas and vitamin deficiency. She tried very hard to keep it clean but after a week in the cells in August 1985, and again in February 1986, she had to shave it off, in the hope of getting the sores cleaned and healed properly. In the spring of 1986, she was expecting a visit from Igor and very much wanted to avoid having a bald head when he came. The KGB told her that Igor was not going to be allowed a visit after all, so she went ahead and shaved it off in order to get the sores under control.

'And what about this flower bed? That sounds odd to me in a prison camp!'

'Yes, it was a bit. It was a little understanding between us and the guards, until Podust got involved,' explained Irina. 'We were only allowed to grow flowers, mind you, not vegetables. Igor couldn't send much in the way of food, but they did let him send seeds for me to grow flowers. But when a seed is a seed you can't tell what it's going to grow into! I got a letter from him one day with some seeds. It said, "These seeds will grow you some nice flowers." I planted them. They did! Cauliflowers!'

'They thought you'd had something to do with a writer called Voloshin, didn't they?'

'Oh yes, that was good! When they searched our flat they found works by Voloshin. So when they tried to interrogate me at the KGB prison after my arrest, they taunted me, "You'd better tell us everything, after all you know your friend Voloshin. Well, yesterday he was sitting in the very same chair where you're sitting, and he told us everything." I should have loved to have told them, Voloshin died in 1932!'

We pulled into Birmingham New Street Station. Michael was there to meet us, and Norma, his wife, had a big bunch of flowers. Two passers-by in the station concourse stopped. 'You're Irina aren't you, the poetess?' The first stop was the synagogue. Rabbi Singer gave Irina an exceptional welcome. 'The Christian Scharansky. The Bright Star of our hope,' he said. Irina had to stay in the women's gallery in keeping with Jewish custom, and Igor came with me. Outside, afterwards, the Rabbi slipped out across the grass to shake her hand and welcome her more personally. We then went on to the Bishop for lunch which was a really happy occasion. Both Bishops were there at the church. Bishop Hugh, his initial reticence gone, joined in with great gusto—true to form. The place was packed. I saw friends there from London, Yorkshire, Wales, Somerset, Oundle, Gloucestershire and all over the country. The Orthodox community came from Bath, and we had some wonderful Eastern singing from them. Bishop Colin's daughter read a poem by Irina:

> Believe me, it was often thus
> In solitary cells, on winter nights
> A sudden sense of joy and warmth
> And a resounding note of love
> And then, unsleeping, I would know
> A huddle by an icy wall
> Someone is thinking of me now
> Petitioning the Lord for me
> My dear ones, thank you all
> Who did not falter, who believed in us!
> In the most fearful prison hour
> We probably would not have passed
> Through everything—from start to end . .
> Our heads held high, unbowed,
> Without your valiant hearts
> To light our path.

Irina and Igor took their places on 'thrones' facing the sea of faces, almost like Canute facing the tide!

After Bishop Hugh's welcome, I made a short speech. I chose to tell the people about Nyurka, which produced a good laugh. I told Irina and Igor that the people of the Midlands really loved them and were so delighted that they'd come and that they were now free.

Bishop Colin then led Irina, Igor and me down to the cell, which we'd constructed for the occasion, and prayed, thanking God for prospering that venture as well as all the others which culminated in Irina's release.

175

The climax came when Colin invited those who had gifts of flowers or those who just wanted to greet them to come forward. The singing started and the crowd surged forward. They kissed her and she kissed them. They embraced Igor, and there were flowers everywhere—just like a carnival! Christopher stood by Irina gazing up at her, just amazed, transfixed in a trance. I think it's the happiest scene I've witnessed in years. Life from the dead! Sue also came up and kissed and greeted them.

I held Christopher in my arms, up there among the bishops! We sang another hymn . . . and processed out to the market-place. A huge banner of Irina draped from the trees. The milling crowd carried us out, gathered all round, and from the vantage point of the shopping centre balcony opposite, called out, 'Irina, Irina. We love you!'

When asked by the media what she thought of it all, Irina replied, 'I am very happy to be here! Thank you all. Remember those who are still in prison.'

> I will survive and be asked:
> How they slammed my head against
> a trestle,
> How I had to freeze at nights,
> How my hair started to turn grey . . .
> But I'll smile. And will crack some joke
> And brush away the encroaching shadow.
> And I will render homage
> to the dry September
> That became my second birth.
> And I'll be asked:
> 'Doesn't it hurt you to remember?'
> Not being deceived by
> my outward flippancy.
> But the former names will detonate
> in my memory . . .
> Magnificent as old cannon.
> And I will tell of the best people
> in all the earth,
> The most tender, but also
> the most invincible,

How they said farewell, how they
went to be tortured,
How they waited for letters
from their loved ones.
And I'll be asked: what helped us to live
When there were neither letters nor
any news—only walls,
And the cold of the cell,
and the blather of official lies,
And the sickening promises made
in exchange for betrayal.
And I will tell of the first beauty
I saw in captivity.
A frost-covered window!
No spy-holes, nor walls,
Nor cell-bars, nor the long endured
pain . . .
Only a blue radiance on one
tiny pane of glass
A cast pattern— none more beautiful
could be dreamt!
The more clearly you looked,
the more powerfully blossomed
Those brigand forests,
camp fires and birds!
And how many times there was
bitter cold weather
And how many windows sparkled
after that one . . .
But it was never repeated,
That upheaval of rainbow ice!
And anyway, what good would it be
to me now,
And what would be the pretext
for that festival?
Such a gift can only be received once,
And once is probably enough.
30 November 1983

EPILOGUE

There's a lot going on in Russia at the moment. It's hard to unravel. Is it momentous or do we heed the person in the street who hasn't yet noticed any difference?

The changes have a genuine feel to them. The homecomings of a hundred prisoners are real and to be welcomed. Mr Gorbachev is to be praised for the courage of his reforms so far. They are very welcome but they must not stop at this point.

In 1965 Leonid Brezhnev became leader of the Communist Party and released large numbers of Christian prisoners. In 1966 almost all were rearrested. In 1955-56 many believers were released on the death of Stalin only to be rearrested two or three years later. May the Gorbachev era bring a more lasting freedom.

He should also reform the courts. Prisoners should be allowed to choose their defence counsel. Their families should be allowed into the courtroom and not excluded by the hordes of workers shipped in by the KGB to pack out the galleries.

Russia needs its religious believers. By and large, they don't steal, they don't get drunk, they work hard and they love their country. If Mr Gorbachev can take the lid off a bit, he will have little cause to regret this injection of new life and new zeal.

But he also needs a change in the law itself. It's very vague and the state can make of it whatever it wants. Anti-Soviet agitation means writing a history of the church, making a list of people who have been arrested, speaking to journalists . . . and you can get fifteen years for it.

Even the laws which do exist are ignored. Many churches try to register with the government but their applications are rejected arbitrarily or postponed for years, forcing them either to meet illegally or to cease to exist. If they do meet, the meetings are raided. The pastors and Sunday school teachers are imprisoned. The congregations are fined heavily and repeatedly and sometimes the building is demolished.

Meeting with your friends at home to talk about God and about living for him can bring a knock at the door and a twelve-year sentence. Okay, the sentence is officially for publishing a magazine. What sort of magazine? Its pages are typed with carbon copies on a rackety old typewriter in somebody's flat. Is the regime really going to fall because of a few pages of typed manuscript circulating hand to hand? The regime seems to fear that it will.

The Bible is printed legally on government presses for the Moscow Patriarchate. Why is it that Baptists who do the same thing are sent to prison? What's wrong with the Bible? It ranks with drugs and pornography in the minds of the customs officers at Moscow airport, so why does the government print it for the Patriarch? The legal version is produced in tiny numbers and is quite inaccessible to the people who want it. Many of the copies end up in closed libraries or are given to visiting delegations to show how much religious freedom there is in the Soviet Union.

Printing of the Bible should be allowed freely in the Soviet Union in whatever quantity the demand dictates. At the moment, people will happily pay £100 for a Bible if they can get their hands on one.

Mr Gorbachev should stamp out the evil practice of confining people in psychiatric hospitals and filling them with neuroleptic drugs to cure them of religious faith or political dissent. In fact, there are signs that he is beginning to do so.

The condition of the prisons is appalling. They will always be needed, but an independent body such as the Red Cross should be invited to inspect them. The new practice of re-sentencing prisoners at the sole discretion of the camp commandant should also be revised.

The inexorable pressure on believers needs to be lifted. Teachers ridicule seven-year-olds for their faith in front of their class-mates. Non-communists can forget about higher education and the professions. Converts in later life fail to advance in their careers or are dismissed. The church leaders are pressurized to rear a church which is mute and docile and a pawn of the government. Active believers are personally slandered in the press with no opportunity to reply. Why should it be this way?

You can't divide politics and religious faith. It's right that Christians should care about their country, and speak up when they think things are wrong.

Any liberalization like this will inevitably bring its problems. As the lid is lifted, some hurtful things will be said about the government. But the government needs to be tolerant enough to sit out the abuse. The old guard will resent losing their privileged status. There should be no witch hunts. Magnanimity and forgiveness are the way forward.

This is no easy task and if Mr Gorbachev pulls it off, the world will be very much in his debt. Let's give him the benefit of the doubt and back him up so long as he works towards these goals.

Some dissidents are nervous of reform. They fear it may be a trap. They wonder how far it will go, how fast and when will be the clamp down. They wonder how a regime openly committed to world domination can ever make real peace with the Western democracies, and therefore ever enjoy real peace within its own frontiers.

Real peace, of course, is not just the absence of war and civil disturbance. It is a state of total well being, total harmony in a land where you can rear your children to be themselves, with nothing and nobody to fear.

Come the day!

In the meantime, don't forget the prisoners.

LIGHT THROUGH THE CURTAIN

Selected and Compiled by
Philip Walters and Jane Balengarth

Christian faith is alive and strong in Eastern Europe. It
has not been extinguished by official atheism.

In this book — through letters, poems, sermons and
stories — some forty Christians give their personal
testaments. They reveal a faith that will inspire readers
everywhere.

Philip Walters is Research Director of Keston College
for the Study of Religion and Communism, the most
respected source of authority on this subject. Jane
Balengarth is a freelance writer.

ISBN 0 85648 784 8

BELIEF IN A MIXED SOCIETY

Christopher Lamb

Western society is now irretrievably mixed and pluralist. In Bradford, a third of babies born are of Asian origin. Thirty schools in the inner city have more than 50 per cent Asian Muslim children. A councillor told a BBC Panorama team: 'We're sitting on a time-bomb here. You've only got to look at the figures to see what the risks are.'

What happens to religious conviction in such a society? Many from Muslim and Hindu backgrounds see the West as bankrupt of moral and spiritual values. Those from a traditional Christian background may be deeply suspicious of the 'threat' of non-Christian cultures.

How far are schools a battleground, how far are they a unifying influence in society? What is the place of religion in schools? How far should we respect different attitudes to women in society, to marriage and the family? Food, health, morality and the law, attitudes to work, to freedom and truth in the media, to wealth and power, all these are areas in which people have to come to terms with those of other faiths or none.

Christopher Lamb writes from personal experience of living in an Asian culture, academic study of Islam and from constant contact with the most pluralist parts of Britain. From 1979 he has been co-ordinator of the Other Faiths Theological Project, run jointly by two Anglican missionary societies. He and his family live in Birmingham, where his wife teaches English to children newly-arrived in Britain.

ISBN 0 85648 210 2

THE LONG ROAD HOME

Wendy Green

She had known for a long time that something was the matter with Peter. But what does a wife do when her husband refuses to communicate and shuts her out? What does she do when her worst fears come true? What does she say to their three teenage children and enquiring three-year-old?

This is a wife's story, the deeply moving record of Peter's last year — and the year that followed. It is full of pain. Yet it touches the heart with warmth. Peter's road home in the end brings healing, perfect, complete. For Wendy the long road continues. With agonizing slowness she leaves behind the valley of shadows, helped by faith and small but certain miracles.

'Let there be new beginnings,' Peter said. A year after his death that almost seems possible.

'The most helpful book I have read since my husband David died... searingly honest.'
Anne Watson

'A brave and hearteningly real book... finally reassuring.'
Mary Craig

ISBN 0 7459 1107 2

SINGLE PARENT

Maggie Durran

'When I left school I was pregnant and soon married.' So begins Maggie Durran's story. Six weeks after the baby was born, the marriage broke down. *Single Parent* is about the next twenty years — the pain, the heartache, and the hope.

This book offers real encouragement to parents who are struggling. With warmth and honesty Maggie Durran looks at the problems of single parenthood and shares her own experience of how a single parent family found its own identity.

Single Parent also gives practical advice on how and where to find help. It's a book for any lone parent, and for anyone concerned to help and understand an increasing number of families in society today.

ISBN 0 85648 848 8

CLEMO — A LOVE STORY

Sally Magnusson

Everything, it seemed, had conspired to make Jack Clemo unmarriageable. Deaf and blind, he lived with his mother in a granite cottage in the dreary shadow of Cornwall's industrial claypits, writing poetry. But the man they called the Poet of the Clay had a dream which nothing could shake. Against all the odds, he believed that his destiny was to marry.

Then in 1967 a letter arrived out of the blue. Painstakingly his mother tapped it out, word by word, on the palm of his hand. 'Dear Jack' it began, and it was signed quite simply 'Ruth'. That letter was to change his life.

This is the moving story of Jack and Ruth Clemo — their extraordinary courtship, their marriage, their faith. It is the story of a love which defied the odds.

Sally Magnusson is well known as a writer and broadcaster. She has presented various BBC television programmes, including *Sixty Minutes*, *Songs of Praise* and *Breakfast Time*. As a journalist she worked on *The Scotsman* and the Scottish *Sunday Standard*. She is also the author of *The Flying Scotsman*, the biography of the Olympic runner Eric Liddell who was featured in the film *Chariots of Fire*.

ISBN 0 7459 1230 3

THE SHADOWED BED

Jack Clemo

'Bert's face became dark and ugly, his arm jerked up —
but it was not to strike. He pulled a red handkerchief from
his pocket and wiped the blood from his cheek.'

In the Cornish claywork village of Carn Veor, sinister,
occult forces are at work among the villagers. Over a
single weekend, when the village is cut off from the outside
world by a landslide, its conflicts reach flash-point. Then
one of the characters central to the designs of evil is
decisively released from its hypnotic hold over her.

In Jack Clemo's powerfully symbolic novel, the
industrial scene takes on cosmic significance as the lives of
the villagers are changed by warring magnetic forces.

'Clemo is the John Bunyan of the century... He is about as
easily digested as hot steel ingots; his power and
importance cannot much longer be evaded.'
Kenneth Allsop

'One of the strangest and most original writers of our time.'
The Sunday Times

'Perhaps the last of the inspired, self-taught, English
working-class visionary writers.'
Evening Standard

ISBN 0 7459 1122 6

RIDERS OF THE COSMIC CIRCUIT

Tal Brooke

Rajneesh is an enigma. Despite ridicule in the popular press, he has drawn thousands of Westerners into his following. What lies at the heart of the magnetic appeal which draws people to the leading gurus?

Tal Brooke shows that their essence is not a new teaching but a new consciousness. Rajneesh, Sai Baba, Muktananda — each has undergone a mind-blowing explosion into a new mode of being. Just what is this 'superconsciousness' and what does it lead to?

The author, Tal Brooke, has held a privileged position in the inner circle of Sai Baba devotees in India. This experience also helped him gain the confidence of members of the Rajneesh ashram in India. His account of these three leading gurus draws some fascinating conclusions.

ISBN 0 7459 1217 6

More stories from Lion Publishing for you to enjoy: